GIRLS WITHOUT A FUTURE

Georgia—who was beaten up on her first date, and had only one aim: to get even with all men.

Jane—the high-priced call girl with only one fear: that she would meet her father on a party.

Betty—the young bride who was launched "in business" by her husband on their honeymoon.

These are some of the New York girls you'll meet in this book, who were willing to tell their whole sordid stories in the hope that other girls might not repeat their mistakes.

A NOTE ABOUT THE AUTHOR

Jess Stearn is a veteran newspaperman who has produced some of the most provocative feature stories of the past twenty years. A native of Syracuse, New York, he attended Syracuse University and at the present time is a reporter on a New York daily.

The people Mr. Stearn has interviewed run the gamut from FDR and Madame Curie to Grace Kelly and Clark Gable. His recent series on juvenile delinquency in the schools brought praise from all over the nation and earned for him the prize of the Silurian Society (the oldest newspapermen's professional group). A subsequent series on narcotics also commanded nationwide attention.

Current **POPULAR LIBRARY** Bestsellers

A CONFIDENTIAL STORY OF BIG-CITY PROSTITUTION

SISTERS
OF THE
NIGHT

JESS STERN

With An Introduction By
PETER E. TERRANOVA

Former Deputy Chief Inspector in
charge of the Police Department's
Narcotic Squad, New York City, and
Member of Governor Harriman's Joint
Legislative Committee on Narcotics

Popular Library   Toronto

POPULAR LIBRARY EDITION
Published in July, 1957

© Copyright 1956 by Jess Stearn
Library of Congress Catalog Card Number: 56-6796

Published by arrangement with Julian Messner, Inc.

Julian Messner, edition published in May, 1956
First printing: April, 1956

Canadian edition published by Copp Clark Company, Ltd.

FOREWORD

Prostitution, the so-called oldest profession, has been an enigma over the centuries.

Its relationship with addiction is well known. Sometimes girls become prostitutes because they need money to buy drugs, having become "hooked" and helplessly dependent on their glass crutch.

On the other hand some prostitutes drift into addiction through contact with addicts or because the procurer may find them easier to deal with if they are addicts.

Jess Stearn, a newspaperman who knows New York City at all levels and is as much at home in a Hell's Kitchen joint as he is at the Waldorf-Astoria, here explores the problem as it exists in America's greatest metropolis. Scorning cheap sensationalism, he asks the question "Why?" more than where and with how many. His girls are representatives of their class—some hopeless, some perhaps smart enough to quit before the inevitable final misery catches up with them.

The old prostitute is fittingly described in the scene in the counter place at night begging $10 until one truck driver looks her over and says in honest bewilderment: "Ten dollars, for what?"

Dorris Clarke, Chief Probation Officer of the Magistrates Courts, who has interviewed more than ten thousand "Sisters of the Night" told Jess of the many girls who would never wind up in Women's Court if it were not for the fact that they were on drugs.

Jess Stearn's approach is both kindly and fair. What can

be done, if anything, for these girls and for the society they threaten?

The work of Girls Term in trying to rehabilitate the neophyte prostitute is ably explained. Countless interviews with police, court personnel, psychiatric experts and the women themselves cast new light on the motivations, way of life and reactions of these girls. Certain inevitable conclusions follow. While the picture is not one of phony optimism, neither is it completely hopeless.

Telling the truth about the problem as it exists today, explaining modern attitudes about it and removing the false shame that surrounds it may well be one of the best ways of starting a move to combat it on a mature and humane level.

Chief Magistrate Murtagh's theory that we are handling the whole matter on a 19th Century basis is skillfully presented and analyzed here. As he points out, vast amounts of money are spent for apprehension and punishment of these women, but not a cent on rehabilitation. Traditional taboos, the policy of keeping the whole matter "under wraps" is as idiotic as the Victorian idea that no nice person knew anything about social disease. When national publicity focused attention on venereal disease, an effective Public Health program was worked out which has greatly reduced the number of initial infections and brought about earlier and more efficient treatment.

Secrecy has a queer way of adding glamor and mystery to a subject. Rip away the Hypocrites' Curtain surrounding prostitution and the whole community will finally recognize that it's just another social evil which may be tackled with intelligence and perhaps cut down, if not completely eliminated.

Both prostitution and narcotic addiction or alcoholism, so often linked in police experience, are symptoms of the same thing—the maladjusted personality, the sick person. Emotionally mature people practically never become addicted, either to drugs or liquor. And certainly, happy, well-adjusted girls from loving homes are not likely to become prostitutes. Some of the human tragedy and waste caused by these aspects of social pathology might be prevented if well-disposed people could be brought to understand the real factors behind them. Besides trying to help those already launched on the prostitute's bitter way of life, whether addicted or not, the community has a responsibility to the unhappy child who will become the prostitute, the drug addict, the alcoholic, the criminal of tomorrow.

Donne's "No man is an island entire to himself" certainly applies here. Well-to-do people with a little time and money to spare could do a lot by befriending a lonely youngster, perhaps through the Big Brothers Movement, the PAL, the Boy Scouts, Girl Scouts or similar agencies.

By furnishing such a mixed-up young person with hope, friendship and a goal in life, thus enabling a child to regain emotional health before one of these scourges take over, furnishing a dubious escape from reality to a private hell from which few escape, an individual could find real satisfaction. This book illuminates the prostitution picture for us. It calls for action!

PETER E. TERRANOVA
Former Deputy Chief Inspector in charge of the Police Department's Narcotic Squad, New York City, and Member of Governor Harriman's Joint Legislative Committee on Narcotics

CHAPTER 1

When I started on what seemed to be a routine assignment, I didn't realize that I was pioneering in a baffling human problem. In fact, it took weeks of investigation for my paper before I recognized how little was actually known about prostitution. And even after my newspaper articles were published, with a gratifying response from the experts, I did not fully understand what makes a prostitute a prostitute.

"The more I explore," I told Chief Magistrate John Murtagh, head of New York's famed Women's Court, "the more I realize how little I understand these women."

The Chief Magistrate smiled sympathetically. "They call it the Oldest Profession," he said drily, "and yet nobody really knows what makes these girls tick.

"The prostitute," he went on, "has never been understood by our courts. Indeed, she is still an enigma to science itself. Because of this lack of scientific knowledge, the degree of moral responsibility is essentially a matter that must be left to the Lord himself."

There were other official indications of the complexities of prostitution. Dorris Clarke, chief probation officer of the Magistrates Courts, who has interviewed more than ten thousand prostitutes, observed with a shrug:

"Psychiatry has been a help, but six different psychiatrists, handling the same case, may still come up with six different answers."

It occurred to me, when I first began thinking about the problem, that prostitution is one of the damning paradoxes of our time. It is a social problem, which cannot be understood apart from other social problems—a postwar deterioration of morality, the alarming increase of dope addiction among teen-agers, political corruption, and the double standard which makes it a crime for a woman to prostitute herself, while her partner in prostitution goes scot free.

Nowhere is prostitution more glittering and glorified than in New York. However, it is prevalent everywhere. An Army colonel, holding commands all over the country, reported from a Texas camp:

"I've never been in a town yet where a man couldn't find a prostitute if he wanted one badly enough."

In New York, flagrant sexual promiscuity, so often the forerunner of prostitution, is obviously increasing, and the "call or cruise" girl working the telephones and the bars, has taken the place of the girl of the streets.

The move to control prostitution legally has been losing ground. The Mayor of Galveston became a celebrity overnight by announcing that he was going to restrict prostitution to red-light districts.

"Christ couldn't prevent it," he said, "so why should I try?"

Long experience has shown that legalization is no remedy. The International Venereal Disease Congress, which voted overwhelmingly thirty years ago for legalized prostitution, recently voted just as overwhelmingly against it.

It was no safeguard, the group found, against VD, for the simple reason that five minutes after she was examined a girl might be infected again.

And the licensing of brothels, the American Social Hygiene Association discovered, makes it easier for girls to begin their careers and forms a convenient center of operations for racketeers and dope pushers.

No, legalization was not the answer, and neither were jails, which became practically schools for prostitutes, where young offenders learned about perversion and dope and became further indoctrinated in the tricks of the trade.

A young graduate of the Women's House of Detention told me that hardly a day passed that older girls didn't approach her looking for drugs. "When I told them I didn't have any," she said, "they'd threaten me."

Other girls assured her that she didn't know what she was missing. "It'll make the slums look like Park Avenue," they promised. And when she got out, she thought she'd try some for kicks. "Any madam or procurer could get it for you."

Some had been given samples by procurers until they became addicted and then found they needed $100 a week to sustain the habit.

"Many of these girls," Dorris Clarke had told me, "would not be in Women's Court if they had not tried to gratifying their cravings for drugs."

In prison, too, many young girls came in contact with Lesbianism for the first time, feeling a response stirring strongly within them as hardened prostitutes sought to reach them with threats or flattery.

No, jail was hardly the place for prostitutes, any more than for alcoholics or addicts. It became obvious to me, as it had long before to Magistrate Murtagh and others, that only a real understanding of these women, of their relationships from childhood, and of their outlook on society and on life in general could lead us to a solution.

Other scourges of Biblical times have been extirpated by modern science—why not prostitution? But first must come understanding, understanding of the girl and her problem.

What, for instance, makes a teen-age girl say sullenly to a probation officer who is trying to help her: "It's my body. Why can't I do with it what I want?"

Or why does another observe slyly:

"If it weren't for us, no woman would be safe on the streets. We're the great outlet."

Why does a girl, able to shift for herself, become attached to a procurer, who mistreats her and takes her money?

And why does still another pin on the wall of her cell a portrait of a muscled brute in loincloth, a whip in one hand, and kneeling behind him in chains a nude girl, arms raised in adoration?

And why does a girl, while bitterly justifying her own prostitution, say with a gleam of hate in her eyes: "I'd kill the man who'd make a prostitute of my sister"?

Or why does a pretty teen-ager, given a separate suite by doting parents, convert her flat into a brothel and then, impenitently, view it all as an ironic joke on her parents?

Why did Anna Swift, one of the most notorious of madams, boast of her virginity and savagely declare she was seeking revenge? (Police, finding all of her twelve girls passing on VD, were quite ready to believe her.)

And why does a former prostitute, comfortably married for years, revert to her old trade at the first crisis in her marriage?

The answers are all in this book and may be a start toward acquainting the public with the real nature of the prostitute. But, meanwhile, as we ponder these questions, hundreds upon hundreds of teen-age girls converge on New York from the forty-eight states—from the slums, from tree-shaded Main Street, from offices and factories, reform schools and finishing schools, all joining the ranks of the Oldest Profession.

While call houses are a thing of the past in New York, the average newcomer finds it easy to begin for herself, or is helped along by small-time racketeers and procurers. To the best of my knowledge, the big-time racketeers, absorbed in the flourishing gambling and dope rackets, have stayed away, cynically, from organizing prostitution.

"It just doesn't pay them enough," one judge declared wryly, "although there are some overlapping interests from the dope traffic and almost any racketeer worthy of the name can pick up the phone at any time of the night or day and get a girl on the double."

This view is supported by Magistrate Murtagh, who has done much toward reforming New York's Women's Court. "You may find a few girls working for one pimp," he declared, "but that's as far as it goes. Even the call-girl racket is not really organized. It's more word of mouth among friends that So-and-so is available for a price."

However, even a small-scale vice operation may read like Big Business. Recently, police smashed a peregrinating ring of pimps which scoured the country for pretty girls and then toured the big cities with them, eventually landing in New York.

In this case, a dozen girls were installed in midtown Manhattan hotels. From the hotels themselves, clerks, bellhops, and elevator operators were recruited to steer the customers—the "Johns" or "meatballs"—to the selected suites.

The fee was $20, standard rate around the country, and many of the girls averaged $100 a night, the group doing better than $6,000 a week, before its arrest, with the girls getting less than one-third as their share.

There is no work too sordid for the pimp. In Brooklyn, men recruited girls from fourteen to sixteen years of age, meeting them in candy stores and near schools, tantalizing them with visions of fine clothes and parties.

The men rented rooms in respectable hotels, on the first floor above the lobby, so that their customers could use the stairways without being seen by elevator men or desk clerks.

It was as smalltime as streetwalking, with a mere $5 fee; the procurer taking $3 of that, and depending on volume for his gain.

I found it useless to talk to these girls. Generally, their intelligence was so low that they not only couldn't grasp my questions, but didn't even begin to understand their own motivations. Even if they had not been prostitutes, they might still have become social problems because of their obvious inadequacies. In the main they were typical—not of a special problem—but of any human being too backward for his environment.

I had to seek out girls with some education, who had given some thought to their own problem, who could discuss it articulately, and who, even in lying, were capable of throwing some light on their problem.

Many of the girls I talked to blamed everything and everyone but themselves for their degradation—a drunken father, being jilted, rape, need to support a child. But time after time, as this justification was offered, I recalled what a well-known analyst had told me: "A girl does not have to become a prostitute because she is unhappy."

A police inspector, who took a bleak view of the whole problem, told me much the same thing in a different way.

"Prostitutes," he said, "form their environment; the environment doesn't form them."

Oddly, of all the people I talked to, virtually only prostitutes and customers took the view that their relationship was the obvious one of supply and demand, with money the prime factor.

Almost without exception, the public officials, psychiatrists, and sociologists I interviewed felt that the underlying causes of prostitution had never been fully explored. They were vitally concerned by the deep-seated motivation of the prostitute. And this was my major concern, too.

"We all know what these girls are doing," my editor had said as he handed me the newspaper assignment. "Find out why they are doing it."

The Oldest Profession held no fascination for me. It was the world's dreariest story and it had been told a thousand times. I wanted no part of it. Prostitution to me meant a motley crew of battered old dames headed for the police lockup and bedraggled streetwalkers searching for any port in a storm.

"Now think back," the editor said, "about your stories on dope and delinquency. Remember all those kids right out of high school who were giving themselves away or selling themselves for peanuts? Don't tell me that they were just out for the money."

"They were delinquents, all right," I said, "or else they were on the junk and didn't know what they were doing or didn't care. They were just crazy kids."

"Okay," he said, "but how about the Jelke girls, the $100 call girls—how crazy are they, and the B-girls that hang around the West Side bars—" Suddenly he broke off. "What's the matter with you? Most of the guys around here would give an arm and a leg to do some original research on this subject." He shook his head. "You're getting old."

I agreed. "Old and respectable. Where do I start?"

"At the source, as on any other story. Get out and talk to the girls, see the judges, the social workers, the cops, the headshrinkers—you won't win a Pulitzer prize but it should be worth reading. Remember," he said as I left the room, "not what, but why."

During years of covering the aches and pains of the city, I had developed contacts on both sides of the law. In no time at all, I must have known more prostitutes than any other man in New York. I met them wherever I could—in bars, night clubs, courts, jails, in their apartments, my office, restaurants, and the street. To some of them, I was just another John cruising from one bar to another, different only because, at the moment of decision, I got up, reached for my hat, and walked out the door. Sometimes I was mistaken for a plainclothesman and then the girls became guarded. But, surprisingly, when I told them that I was a reporter frankly trying to find out what makes them tick, they were only too eager

to talk. Sometimes I was screened by pimps and procurers and, as a reporter, pledged to forget names and
faces. I had little trouble getting in touch with even the
high-priced Park Avenue call girls who were so afraid
of exposure that they dated only men with references.

The stories the girls told me were often poignant,
sometimes tragic, seldom dull. Many of them looked so
innocent that it was often hard to realize I was actually
talking to a prostitute and that she was telling me her
story.

Sometimes it was embarrassing to sit through these
interviews as women relived the anguish of their most
intimate moments. But, strangely enough, they themselves
never showed the slightest embarrassment or remorse.
Frequently, resentment crept into their voices and, occasionally, I caught them appraising me quietly, obviously speculating whether my professional blandness
would desert me under direct assault.

In my office one afternoon, a $100 call girl, an attrac-
tive, articulate blonde of twenty-six, told me that some
Johns call for two girls a day. She leaned over the carriage
of my typewriter.

"These Johns are real degenerates."

I must have lifted my eyebrows, because the girl looked
me up and down and said:

"You seem like a normal guy. You ought to know
about things like that."

I commented tersely that I had never consulted a prostitute for reasons other than information.

"In that case," she said scornfully, "you must be a
degenerate, too."

Even when she appears to prosper, as did this girl, the
prostitute leaves a trail of heartbreak, usually her own.
At best, she moves only in a mirage of glamour. She has
no present or future, only a past which took with it
the only niceness she ever knew.

She can be of almost any age or from any background.

She may be sixteen or sixty-five, a motherless girl or a minister's daughter, a recent virgin or a housewife with children.

Outlawed herself, she is still part of the legitimate commerce of a great city, hired by respectable businessmen to impress and entertain equally respectable customers.

She is a familiar—and welcome—figure in the exclusive Fifth Avenue shops and she is also well known in Women's Court, where hundreds like her turn up penniless each year, too destitute to hire a lawyer for their defense.

Their lives appear dedicated to fun and frivolity, and yet how often had I observed them in moments of despair. I had seen some of them dining gaily in New York's smart supper clubs and later learned of their suicides.

They are usually on the brink of emotional upheaval. One of the first girls I met—a nineteen-year-old brunette —had been talking calmly about her parents and home when she suddenly went into a frenzy of rage.

"I hate them all!" she cried. "They're all pigs. I give them as little as I can and take as much as I can. I cheat them whenever I can and wherever I can, and I'm only sorry when I don't get away with it."

The interview had been set up by an intermediary, a pear-shaped, small-time racketeer named Dick (whom I had long suspected of being a procurer). I paid him to arrange the meeting and he came along to handle the introductions and also, I surmised, to keep posted.

En route, he told me that Jean had been in the business for only six months and was getting $25 a call, but that eventually she would earn up to $50 or $100.

"She's from a small town," he confided in a whisky whisper, "and needs brushing up. When she learns to make with the fancy talk the rich Johns like she'll be in the dough. But she's got to get around more."

Warning me that the girl was moody, he added reassuringly: "She'll get over that; she's new at the game."

Jean received us courteously. She looked like a student or secretary, simply dressed in a suit that failed to conceal her shapeliness. She wore no jewelry and no make-up except lipstick and eyeshadow.

As she took my coat, I looked around the living room. It was comfortable and simple. There was a large davenport at one end, two upholstered chairs at the other. There were a few small tables, a radio-phonograph, a television set, but what caught my eye was a small crucifix on the wall over the couch. It was the only ornament in the room.

The girl noticed my glance.

"This is my retreat," she said. "Nobody has been here except friends. I never bring anybody home with me." Although she put no stress on the word, it was clear what she meant by *anybody*.

"This," she said, "is where I try to forget."

Jean mixed a couple of Scotches, looked over at me, ignoring Dick, and said:

"You wanted to ask a few questions. Well, ask."

I had not expected her to be so matter-of-fact. "Tell me anything you like," I said. "It's mostly background I'm concerned with. I'd like to know how you got"—I hesitated—"the way you are now, but I don't want to pull you apart."

She reached for a cigarette, settled back in her chair, crossed her slim bare legs, and took a deep drag on the cigarette. She seemed amused, certainly not disconcerted.

"I suppose I should start at the beginning. That's where all sad stories start, isn't it?"

Her voice was soft and clear. She seemed completely absorbed in her own story, almost as though she were listening, too, but when she began talking about how she had fallen in love, her dark eyes became cloudy.

"He was separated from his wife and had promised to marry me," she said. "It was the same old story, but I believed it." She laughed. "How silly can you get, believing a man."

She made a face, as though she had tasted something unpleasant.

"You know, I don't think the man ever lived you could trust. They're all alike. I trusted this guy and what did it get me? One night he gave me the routine. I kept saying I wanted to wait."

She crushed her cigarette into an ashtray. "It's hard to believe, I suppose, but I was a virgin then, hardly seventeen, and he forced me."

Dick was moving restlessly in his chair. "How could he force you?" he asked. "No man can force a girl." He looked to me for support. "Isn't that right?"

I shrugged.

She gave Dick a withering look, then turned to me. "I tell you," she cried, "he forced me!" With her well-manicured hands she gripped her throat and started to squeeze until the blood rushed to her head. Her breath came in gasps.

"That," she panted, "was how he choked me. But I fought back. I bit, I kicked, I scratched, I even used my knee on him. When he hit me, I kept fighting, until he got out handcuffs and slipped them on me. He was a cop; he came prepared." She brushed her arm over her eyes. "After that, I must have passed out."

Suddenly the tears streamed down her face.

I thought it was time to end the interview. But Dick, who had been eying her unsympathetically, said gruffly:

"She'll be all right. She upsets easy."

Jean's head came up angrily. She sprang to her feet and began pacing the floor like a caged animal.

"Upsets easy!" she cried. "So I'm upset easy." She faced him furiously. I thought for a moment she was going to strike him. "Do you know what it is to walk down the street and be ashamed to look up, to be ashamed to look into a mirror, to feel so dirty you can never get clean again?"

She pointed to the wall. "See that crack in the plaster?" she cried. "That's where I banged my head the night I became a whore."

This was when she had screamed: "I hate them all! They're all pigs!"

She stood there, legs and arms tense, as though waiting for one of us to challenge her. There was a harsh ring to her voice. She couldn't have stopped talking now if she had wanted to. She seemed to be trying to prove something.

I thought I'd try to find out what it was.

"I guess you were forced, all right," I said tactfully, "but nobody forced you into the business, did they?"

"Wherever I went," she said, "men would never leave me alone. When I came to New York, the cab driver had a hotel to take me to. The bellhop had people he wanted me to meet. When I went for a job, they kept asking why I wanted to be a secretary. They wanted me to lift my skirt and show my legs.

"They kept telling me I was a fool to work for fifty a week, when I could make five hundred—easier."

She nodded scornfully in Dick's direction. "And when I was making five hundred, they tried taking that, too."

Why didn't she give it up if she hated men so much?

"You're young and pretty—nobody would know what you've been doing. Why don't you go away and make a fresh start?"

"It would be the same wherever I went. It's got inside me. I'm not like other girls any more."

"How about getting married?" I asked.

"There isn't a man I'd ever give myself to," she said. "No man gets anything from me. I get to feeling dead. Nothing matters. And I think of what they've done to me."

Then her face lit up. Her voice rang out: "That's what

keeps me going, the thought of getting even. I'll never get out until I'm even with the whole rotten lot."

She was sobbing when I left, and Dick was hovering about helplessly. It was like walking out of a bad dream.

But even in the sanity of the street bits of it kept coming back, bits that didn't seem to fit anywhere. Other parts of the jigsaw kept jamming my brain, trying to form some kind of pattern. Finding out "why" wasn't going to be as simple as I had thought.

The only thing I was sure about then was that the prostitute is no more like other women than a zebra is like a horse. She is a distinct breed, more different from her sisters-under-the-skin than she—or the rest of society—could possibly realize.

I have overheard prostitutes sneering about the degeneracy of males and contemptuously branding them as animals. And yet in dime-a-dance halls, I have seen dime-a-dozen girls pressing closely against their male dancing partners and sighing:

"This is only a sample, brother. Meet me later and try the whole bottle."

The prostitute reflects the callous sophistication of an indifferent city. At two o'clock one morning I followed a streetwalker as she crept, dirty and disheveled, into a dingy restaurant in upper Manhattan and tried to sell herself for $10 to the men at the counter.

"Ten dollars," a beefy truck driver frowned, looking her up and down, "ten dollars—for what?"

The other men laughed.

She went from man to man, finally asking 75 cents. The counterman made a move to throw her out, when a customer handed her a hamburger and pushed her, not ungently, out the door.

"Send your daughter next time," another man called after her. And everybody laughed.

And the next day, as I interviewed a sleek redheaded call girl in her fashionable East Side apartment, I wondered how many men it would take, how many beatings, how many sleepless nights before she lost the youth and resilience that stood between her and the creature I had seen the night before.

Her lovely face was discolored and there was a small mouse on one eye. These were the souvenirs of a wealthy playboy who gave her a retainer of $200 a week just to be available for his beatings.

Why should a beauty, who could tempt almost any man, submit to this treatment?

I remember her flip. "It pays well."

"But why," I persisted, "does he do it?"

She shrugged. "I suppose," she said casually, "because he likes it. Maybe it makes him feel like a man."

There were many other things that puzzled me at first, including the prostitute's attitude toward marriage. Even when she does marry it is only an incident in her life.

I met a mother of three who had recently rewarded a broad-minded husband with a Cadillac convertible. "When we save enough," she said, "we're getting a home in the country."

Outside a Manhattan courtroom I spotted a teen-ager with gold dust in her eyes and a summons to a vice case in her purse.

"Why," I asked, "doesn't a girl like you get married and have a flock of kids?"

She shrugged.

"How could anybody lie next to the same man all night?"

I have interviewed call girls who had spurned offers of marriage from men of wealthy and prominent families because it would have meant giving up the pimps and procurers to whom they were attached. And, while other women view abortion as a catastrophe, I have heard prostitutes discuss them gaily, one telling me that she had had a dozen and would probably have a dozen more.

"Children," she grimaced, "are such miserable monsters."

Almost any conclusion I reached about these girls was subject to change as I continued my research. They turn to dope, and yet under its influence completely lack interest in sex. Their main asset is youth, yet they toss it away on drink and drugs. They claim not to care what others think, but are shattered by exposure. But, despite the fact that they operate in many different ways, they have one common denominator, one essential quality that distinguishes each of them from other women—a profound contempt for the opposite sex.

CHAPTER 2

"When you learn what makes these girls tick," the Inspector said, "let me know—that'll make two of us."

The inspector could have located any call girl in town within a few hours but, grown tolerant with the years, was resigned to prostitution as an inevitable evil.

"As long as there's men around buying," he said, "there's going to be girls selling. It's the pimps and madams I'm after, the jackals that live off these poor girls and grab half their take."

"Poor girls?"

"Yes, poor girls. I know cops have hearts of stone, but if I have sympathy for anyone, it's for these girls."

"Why do they need madams?" I asked.

"These girls get the feeling they don't matter to anybody," he said. "The madam plays on all their fears and insecurities and makes them feel important." He shrugged. "Too bad we can't get the madams without getting the girls. But you have to grab them in the same bag. It's the girl who leads us to the madam."

He leaned back in his chair. "We landed an old-time madam the other day. I'd been after her for years. She finally made the mistake of mentioning money over a tapped line. We picked up two girls in the raid. You should have seen them—a blonde and a brunette. They were knockouts. I'll bet you never saw two better-looking girls in your life—both about twenty-two, the kind any young fellow would go nuts about. I've seen a lot in my forty years in the department, but these kids beat anything yet. You just can't tell a book by the cover any more. They don't wear make-up, they stare at you with those wide eyes of theirs, and with their skirts and sweaters and saddle shoes they look as if they had just stepped off a college campus.

"And do you know what?" he added. "Some of them have. I had a pair in here the other day and I felt like apologizing to them—they looked so sweet and pure. So I watch the way I talk in front of them, and they talk back to me like prostitutes."

Many of these girls, I had learned myself, had drifted into prostitution from the easy promiscuity of Manhattan's West Side bars. Touring these honkytonk bars night after night, from eleven o'clock, when they begin to crowd up, until three or four in the morning, when they close, I had met the B-girls. Occasionally I was accompanied by an H-man (an investigator from the United States Public Health Service), whose job it was to track down carriers of venereal disease.

The B-girls (B for bar) converge on Manhattan from all over the nation, but many are native New Yorkers. They boast of their "amateur standing" and prefer servicemen, who usually pay them nothing, to civilians, who are prepared to offer liberal rewards.

"All we can do about those B-girls is keep them moving," the Inspector said, "and then they find another bar someplace else. A lot of them start at sixteen, and if they don't make the grade by the time they're twenty-five they're out in the streets ready to settle for anybody."

At this point the Inspector was called out of the room, leaving me with my own recent recollections of B-girls. It had not been difficult to get them to talk. Like other prostitutes, they were willing to converse freely with me as long as they were not identified by name.

"We don't take money for ourselves," a teen-ager told me in a bar near Times Square. "I've helped out sailors more than they've helped me. But if they have money and want to leave it for the rent or a new dress, that's different."

A surprising number of B-girls evinced a clinical interest in their own problem. In a small bar near Madison Square Garden an attractive blonde, trying to analyze her endless hopping from bar to bar said: "I guess I'm typical, but I've probably thought more about it than the others—my brother is a psychiatrist and I guess analysis runs in the family."

She had been standing at the bar with a group of other girls when I came in. When I offered to buy her a drink, the bartender looked questioningly at the bouncer, who nodded, and then set up the drinks. After another round or two, the other girls and the bouncer disappeared, leaving me alone with the blonde, who was obviously taking my measure while chattering away about herself.

She was about nineteen years old and had run away from her family in West Virginia. Her hair was done up in a chignon, apparently to make her look older. She wore a print dress cut low at the neckline, and her shoulders still revealed traces of a summer tan. She shifted restlessly about on the stool, crossing and uncrossing her legs, causing her skirt to flutter above the knee. Frequently she would lean forward to confirm, I am sure, that nature had endowed her generously. Even the hazards of her occupation had not yet dimmed her healthy glow.

While still concentrating on me her eyes shifted appraisingly to each newcomer. Two young sailors passed enroute to the rear of the bar; she greeted them cheerfully and called out, "See you later." Then she turned back to me. "They say a lot of girls are uniform-crazy," she said. "Well, maybe, but it's deeper than that. With sailors there's not much chance of getting hurt. They're on the go and so are we. Maybe that's the attraction—what the Spanish girls call *simpatico*. I wouldn't be interested in soldiers or sailors if I cared about money, would I? I've taken many a sailor who was down and out to my room. I might have spent the night with a boy from Princeton and done myself some good, but I didn't."

"Isn't it a problem," I asked, "bringing young men to your room night after night."

"I live in a hotel," she explained, "where they let people live their own lives."

"Don't you ever become attached to any of these boys?"

"It all depends what you mean by attached. I like to hear from them. It gives you a nice feeling to get a letter from some far-off country." She laughed. "Some of the girls save the stamps, and we trade from our collections when we get duplicates. Whenever their buddies get in town, they look you up, too. That makes it really interesting—new faces all the time."

She puffed on her cigarette, blowing a blue smoke ring into my eye. "You know," she said, as though the thought had just occurred to her, "you're asking an awful lot of questions. You must be a reporter or something like that, but it must be all right or the bartender would have had the bat out long ago."

She dropped the cigarette to the floor, crushed it with her foot, and said: "I want you to know one thing, Mr. Reporter. I'm not a tramp. I work hard during the day. I'm a clerk in a factory. It's damn dull, and the nights are the only thing that keep me alive. I know I can't go on like this forever, but I'll worry about the future when it gets here."

Her voice rose harshly. "The only thing that burns me is these people that think they're better than we are. Who the hell are they to talk?"

She finished her drink and motioned to the bartender for another.

"My morals are as good as any girl's. I don't care

whether she's a secretary, an actress, a society girl, or what. Everybody knows what a girl has to do to get anywhere in the theater, for instance. What difference does it make what you sell yourself for?

"And how about the society girls who marry older men they don't love—who just *happen* to have money? *I'll* say they're different from us. At least we don't take home anybody we don't like. What about those people who mess around country clubs? One of the girls got an invite to a dance at a yacht club in Connecticut, and a man came up to her, drooling, and said it was too bad she wasn't married; this was wife-swap night, and he wanted to swap for her."

Mollified by my silence, which she took for agreement, she became somewhat calmer. "My parents," she said in a much lower voice, "were so religious they didn't like me seeing boys. I couldn't even bring a boy home after I got to be sixteen. I began meeting them on the sly at bars. My parents thought I was at a girl friend's. I picked out a girl that didn't have a phone, so they couldn't check on me. If they had let me bring some of those monsters home, I'd probably have lost interest in the whole thing."

She smiled bleakly. "When they found out, boy, did Pop raise a storm! That's when I decided to clear out. I had some money saved up, so I got a bus ticket, kissed Mom goodbye, and beat it. I didn't even look at my father."

She glanced over her shoulder at the couples kissing and fondling each other in the booths and swaying to a jukebox on the tiny floor.

"Some real big romances get started here," she said proudly. "Some of these girls are as nice as you'll meet anywhere. They work in insurance offices and other big companies, but don't get to meet the right fellows. I know two girls who married GIs they met here and two more are engaged.

"There's no saying how long these things'll last, but at

least they're married now. Believe me—" she pressed her hands to her bosom—"believe me, we're not as bad as some people paint us. I've never known a B-girl who's taken anybody unless he had it coming."

"How about the girls who get arrested for rolling drunks in bars?" I asked.

"They're not B-girls—they're nothing but plain old prostitutes, that's what. Sure, some of us accept money, but only when we're broke. We're not asking anything for what we're ready to give away. And if we're not willing to give it away, we won't sell it for any price. How many girls on Park Avenue can match that record?"

With that, she scrambled off the barstool. "So long, Mr. Reporter," she said, and dashed off to join her sailor friends.

At another bar, not far away, the scene was virtually the same, except that most of the girls looked older and there were fewer uniforms. The young girls and the uniforms seemed to go together.

I was sitting at the end of the bar when an emaciated-looking brunette lurched up to me and said, "I'm Marie, honey. Can I sit here?"

She was hardly settled when a waitress suggested we take a booth in the back. "Just right for the two of you," she said.

The activity was now familiar. The unattached B-girls were clustered together in small groups, turning expectantly toward the door with each new arrival. The others were giving their wholehearted attention to soldiers or sailors, a privilege they rarely accorded to civilians unless they were Marie's age and could no longer be choosy.

One unattractive teen-ager with acned skin was scribbling her phone number for a sailor. In another booth a clean-cut girl of about eighteen was embracing another sailor whom she fondly called "Mate."

"What's a youngster like that doing in here?" I wondered out loud.

Marie gave me a searching look. "What the hell," she said, "you out for a good time or writing a book?"

It was a good question, but silence, I had discovered, was the surest way to gain a prostitute's confidence.

Marie was obviously on the decline at thirty. She consumed whisky faster than I could order it. At last she was ready to talk. "You know," she said, "I wasn't always like this. I was decent once."

It was the same story, though not so complex, as Jean's. There was the usual man who had treated her shabbily. "I was working at a post exchange when I met The Soldier," she recalled. "We started seeing each other regularly. One night he told me he loved me and was going to divorce his wife. That was the first I knew he was married.

"He was so upset that he started to cry, and I tried to comfort him. That was the first time I stayed with him. When he went overseas he promised to write every day. I got three letters in three months, and that was it. Guess my Ex, as I called him, must have spread some great stories about me because I certainly became popular with a lot of other soldiers after that."

As I watched her down another rye-on-the-rocks I asked when she had started to drink so heavily.

"I don't drink much," was her reply, "just when I get to thinking about things."

She looked up and muttered drunkenly, with a grotesque effort at gaiety, "To hell with The Soldier. Let's live it up a little."

As I left, her raucous voice echoed shrilly in my ears. She was saying, over and over again, "To hell with The Soldier—one more on the rocks."

I had had my fill of bars for the night but, passing a tavern off Times Square, I spotted three teen-agers through the window and went in. They were sitting in a booth and the most attractive of the three, a redhead, had a warm smile for the few stragglers at the bar. She was so lovely that I wondered how her two friends had a chance with her around. She had a cute, turned-up nose, lightly ██████████████ radiant blue eyes, and a wonderful complexion.

I asked the waitress if the girl would join me for a drink. The girl nodded with an engaging smile and came to the bar immediately. Her two friends soon finished their drinks and disappeared.

Alice was completely at ease, and without prompting told me about the men she had met, the places they had taken her, the movies she liked, and the shows she wanted to see. She wouldn't tell me her age, but she could hardly have been more than eighteen.

She lived in a furnished room near Broadway. "It's not much," she said, "but nobody bothers me. Now tell me about yourself—where do you live?"

I told her I was new in the city and hadn't found a place yet. "That's too bad," she sympathized, and promptly pulled a door-key out of an oversized pocketbook.

"That," she remarked airily, "is the key to my heart— and my room."

"Do you do this often?" I inquired.

"I must have heard that question a hundred times," she laughed. Then she said more seriously:

"When you go out to buy a pair of shoes, do you always buy the first pair you try on? Of course not. You keep looking until you find the pair that fits. When a girl goes out with some boy and finds out that he's not right, you can hardly blame the girl for getting rid of him. That's why she's got to try them all before she finds the one she wants. How else can she be sure?"

"Sorry I was so long," the Inspector said as he came back into the room. He shuffled through some papers on his desk, glanced at his watch, and then looked at me over his glasses. "Where were we?" he asked. "About through?"

I smiled. "I don't know where you were, but I was in

a bar off Times Square and not quite believing it. Can't something be done about these kids ▓▓▓▓▓▓▓▓▓▓▓▓

He shrugged. "By the time they've reached the bars it's already too late. All we can do is close a place if they serve under-age kids. So we sweep them out of one place, and they turn up in another. We close one place, and another opens up. I'm not passing the buck, believe me, but basically it's not a police problem—it's a human problem."

I got up to go. "Maybe I'll check back with you, Inspector. A couple of your detectives have a diary I want to look at. They picked it up in a narcotics raid. They call it the story of the girl who never had a chance."

CHAPTER 3

As I leafed through the diary, a valentine fell to the floor. I picked it up. There were two hearts pierced with an arrow. It read, "To Peggy, with Love, From Steve."

There were other little enclosures: a restaurant menu inscribed, "My first dinner date with Tom"; program notes from a symphony concert at Carnegie Hall; two ticket stubs from the Capitol Theatre.

The detective who handed me the diary was a college-trained sophisticate of thirty-five. "I wouldn't get too sentimental if I were you," he said. "We get these things all the time."

"Mind if I run through it more carefully?" I asked.

"Keep it," he said. "We took down about everything that mattered—the kids she knocked around with, where she went for the junk, and that sort of thing."

Peggy's handwriting was barely legible. "Is there anything I should know that isn't here?" I asked.

"It all depends what you're looking for," he said. "She was an average kid, seventeen, not particularly pretty. A little surly, but you can't tell by that. She might have been scared. As I recall it, it was her first arrest."

I settled back in a comfortable chair and began to read:

Jan. 1
Dear Diary:
I came in this afternoon at four o'clock, I had been with Tom all night. To be truthful, diary, it was the most wonderfulest New Years I ever had. Well, when I got home Daddy had cut the fool and swelled Mom's eye and

33

everything. Tomorrow Mom and I are going to get a warrant for his arrest. To avoid confusion, Mom's staying with a friend and I'm at Jean's. We met Frank and Smitty and talked about Shakespeare, etc., then Frank showed us the adding machine they stole (it's a beauty). I had my first coke [cocaine]. They called it C. It made me sick.

Jan. 2

Mom called this morning and we went downtown to the Tombs. Her eye, by the way, went down a great deal. The court was closed, so we'll have to get the summons tomorrow. We went home, but since Daddy was there we went to Mrs. Mack's house. I met Tom but I didn't like him tonight because he was too fresh. Got a letter from Steve.

Jan. 3

Jean and I didn't get up until late. Tom and Frank came up. We cooked dinner and they ate with us, then we went to listen to records and talk. You know, diary, I'd give anything to know how Tom feels about me.

Jan. 4

Jean and I got up early yesterday to go look for a job, but because it was such a beautiful day we went downtown to the show. I really enjoyed myself tonight. Tom is so sweet. The cops served Daddy the summons today.

Jan. 5

Tom called. In ways, diary, to be truthful, Tom moves me a great deal. I only hope it doesn't develop into anything serious, because I know with all my heart there will never be another boy for me except Steve. Tom, by the way, is having a picture taken for me.

Jan. 6.

Today was a very special day for me because I am going

home. Daddy sounded pitiful over the phone. Even so, I can't stand him. Tom is not taking me to the show tonight because he has a deal coming up at 11:30. I don't know, diary, he's getting so you can't count on him for anything.

Jan. 7

Tom told me the reason why he doesn't take me out was because I had Jean with me and he didn't like it. He, by the way, had plenty of money tonight.

Jan. 8

I had a date with Larry at six. We went downtown to the Roxy, then to Marco Polo to dinner and what a dinner. It was a three-course meal. My dinner, by the way, cost $2. Larry, by the way, wants me to forget Steve. Is he kidding (he must be!)?

Jan. 9

Tom finally called and to my surprise he had a half pint of gin, ginger ale, ice and my favorite cigarettes. We drank, smoked, kissed, danced, etc., all in all having a wonderful time. Mom dropped the warrant against Dad.

Jan. 10

Tom told me that he had an argument with Frank last night, and Frank told him I was getting engaged. Tom asked me if it was true and of course I said yes. You should have seen his face!

Jan. 11

I got a letter from Steve tonight and, diary, he really means it about getting engaged. I know when this happens, I will be good, but right now I have to have my fun. I only hope Steve will understand when he comes home.

Jan. 12

I went to the candy store to listen to records. I had Steve's picture with me. And, diary, while listening to the records, I felt so lonely and empty inside. Later Tom met me and brought me home. We had some pot [marijuana] together. It's a help. All the garbage cans seem to disappear.

Jan. 13

I'm worried about Tom. He didn't show up until two. His hair was all mussed up, his pants were bloody, his hands cut. Someone had stuck him up and stole his coat and he had to fight his way out. Tom and Frank went back with guns but didn't see anybody.

Jan. 14

It was wet home tonight. Jean came by and Mom was high. She gave Jean and me a shot of Carstairs. Then Daddy came home. He was drunk, so he started fussing about Jean being there all the time. So we went over to Jean's house. Hell, diary, Jean's mother was also high and we sat around drinking brandy. Everyone was feeling fine. But no one was feeling as fine as Frank, he wanted Jean to go to a hotel with him (how fine can he get).

Jan. 15

Dear Diary:

What a hangover!!!

Jan. 16

I still don't feel very well. Tom came over with Frank. We went into one room while Jean and Frank stayed in her room. We were lying on the bed talking and kidding around. Honestly, diary, I never laughed so much at one boy in my life, he kept me in hysterics at the things he was doing.

Jan. 17

Today I just don't feel like being bothered with Tom and Frank. In fact, you might say I am tired of them. After all, I am almost a married woman and that *just ain't right*. Tom had two tickets to see Hamlet, $1.20 each. I wonder who he is taking?

Jan. 18

Today I got sick, but I would have been sicker still if I hadn't. Because of that I have been in bed all day.

Jan. 19

We got over to Jill's about ten. Had gin and beer. We're supposed to go over again tomorrow because six of us girls are supposed to get high on tea.

Jan. 20

The party didn't come off. Jill cut out on us.

Jan. 21

Yes, diary, I have started all over again. I invited Tom to dinner. Then we went to Jean's party. Tom had seven sticks of pot and turned us all on. Everyone was high and we all had a fine time.

Jan. 22

We went to the Gardens (the four of us) and had many drinks. We had fun on the way, for I was Ophelia, Jean, Cleopatra, Tom, Samson, and Eddie, Hamlet. Then we got mad at them and walked by ourselves and guess what—this drunk thought we were whores. Jean and I led him on. But when we told him it would be more than a measly $10 each, he swore we were not even whores. So we laughed in his face and went on. At Eddie's we listened to records, danced and kissed. Forgive me, Steve, but Tom sure can kiss.

Jan. 24

Well, I got my long-awaited letter from Steve and do you know, diary, he avoided the money matter very well. I sent him a telegram saying we are through and I mean it, too. From now on, I'm looking out for little Peggy.

Jan. 26

Oh, yes, I am now letting Tom wear my ring. He wants me to help him pass out the pot. I could use the money.

Jan. 30.

You know, diary, I got a letter from Steve and he still loves me. He sent a money order. I really don't deserve him. He's too sweet. It's about time I did what he wanted me to for a change.

Jan. 31

I sent Steve another telegram today. I hope everything is okay now.

Feb. 1

We played records, danced, drank beer, and talked. Then Tom did something he never did before. I was really getting my kicks when Harry came in.

Feb. 2

Tom's in trouble again. When I saw him, his face was red, his shirt dirty, and his coat torn. You see, diary, he had just come out of jail. Last night in a bar on the East Side he had an argument. This man pulled a knife on him, so he shot at him, but hid the gun. Because he had no weapon, he only stayed one night.

Feb. 3

Diary, I really enjoyed myself last night. Tom sure can upset a person. We drank and smoked our pot without offering anybody any. I was high as high could be so I went and laid down on Tom's bed, for my mind was on him and not Steve.

Feb. 5

Tonight Tom heard about a new connection for dope and stopped into a bar. Frank and I waited outside. This Spanish guy came up and talked to Frank. Do you know, diary, he thought I was a whore?

Feb. 6

Frank told me Jill was going to start working for Harry. She starts tonight. Harry's girl will show her the ropes. After Jill makes good, she won't have to go in the street, she'll be a call girl then and meet the right people.

Feb. 7

Jill went downtown last night, but changed her mind at the last minute. She said she's going to give it another try tomorrow night.

Feb. 9

Jill and I tried to talk Harry into buying us a bottle of gin. In fact, we almost did, but he figured he should get something in return. He said we could make a team. I got mad.

Feb. 10

Today Tom and I had a very interesting conversation on sex, and being sterile. Tom, by the way, says it's hard for him to understand me. In fact, he wanted to know just what our relationship was. I told him he was my friend and he got sassy. [You know, diary, I aroused him so much today, he didn't want me to leave.]

Feb. 13

I put Steve's picture and mine in the locket he gave me. It looks very well. You know, diary, I'm really going to

stop fooling around this time because I am not being fair
to Steve. People actually believe I go with Tom, which
isn't good, for my heart is in California with Steve.

Feb. 14
I didn't even receive a valentine from Steve. Some sweetheart I got. I stopped by Jill's and she hinted she was in
business. Mom thinks I ought to do something about a
job.

Feb. 16
Daddy bought a pint of whisky and before he left for
work the three of us had a drink. After a while I went
uptown to my aunt's. She has a bar and, diary, I didn't do
anything but drink whisky and beer, for since I was a
relative, I got everything free.

Feb. 17
You know Tom hasn't called me yet. Well, if he wants to
see me that's the only way he will, because I decided to
turn over a new leaf and really be true to my supposingly
fiancé.

Feb. 23
Oh, yes, diary, Tom's back.

Feb. 24
I finally got to the dance and if I do say so myself I didn't
look so bad. I had a fine time. You know, diary, I was so
high tonight. Everybody had a table with plenty to drink.
Tom came in late as usual. Anyway the dance was over
at three. Tom sure was sweet.

Feb. 25
Have a hangover to beat all hangovers. Guess it was that
cigar Tom and I smoked last night (ugh). I stopped up at
Steve's house to see his mother. She, by the way, is sick.

March 1

Tom came over. He, by the way, doesn't think I should get married. Between you and me, diary, I think Tom thinks I like him a hell of a lot (excuse me). He also said he wished I was older (I wonder why). Before leaving he asked me for Steve's address. I gave it to him, too (calling his bluff).

March 2

I stopped by Tom's, for he told me to come up as he had something to tell me, but as usual it was all a bluff to get me up there.

March 3

Steve's mother called. She said he called her Thursday night and guess what—he lost all his money gambling. Steve is getting on my nerves, he just didn't want to send me the money. I was so disgusted I went up to Tom's house. I had the nerve to wear my dungarees and shirt, too. I really had fun with him.

March 4

Walking to the bus, Jill and I met this fellow. He bought us a gang of drinks, plus cigarettes and nickels for the jukebox and when we were going home he gave me $1 for cab fare. We got out and started walking again. A fellow picked us up and he had the nerve to ask us if we were out for sport. We laughed and went on. Mom's mad because I haven't done anything about a job.

March 5

Jill called, she had made a date with the cab driver last night. The fellow was standing outside waiting for us. We went in and had a couple of drinks. Then he started acting like a fool. So the bouncer told him we were too young and we all had to leave. Anyway we couldn't get rid of him so we took him to this bar and got him drunk.

We met a lot of fellows but when they tried to take his money, we left quick.

March 7

Tom was sweet tonight. Only thing, he scared the hell out of me with his gun.

March 8

Tom sure is acting funny. Well, he doesn't have to worry for I won't bother him any more. From now on if he wants to see me, he'll have to call me and this time I mean it. As the old saying goes, "Experience is the best teacher." Oh yes, Mom's going to give me money to register for a job on the 20th (I sure am glad).

March 10

This afternoon when I got up, guess what came—my valentine candy from Steve. It's in the most beautiful heart-shaped box you'd ever want to see. I guess I'm just about the luckiest girl in the world and have the swellest boy friend, too. Oh, how I love that boy. I most certainly am going to marry him. He's just about the best. And I, above anyone, should know.

March 11

Talked to Steve's mother. She was very happy for me, and told me to be good to her son. I promised her I would and that's one promise I am going to keep. For she said Steve thinks a whole lot of me and it would hurt him if anything goes wrong.

March 14

We all played cards at Jill's. After they finished with whist, they started playing strip poker. I was playing Frank at first and he was losing his clothes. In fact, he got stark naked. But when I started playing Jack, that's where I began to lose my clothes. Naturally, tho, I had a blanket. After all, my virtue! Tom came over and walked me home. He was giving out with the kisses (so much affection). I swear I was never so disgusted in all my life.

March 15

Jean and I went to the party. All the fellows were there. Everyone was telling me how healthy I looked, etc., and Dick told me Steve is going to be proud of me when he comes home.

March 16

Wrote Steve and read some of his letters. I should get a letter from him tomorrow, no later than Sat. You know, diary, I don't think I could ever love anyone the way I love Steve. For there is no shame for me where he is concerned. While looking at his picture, I am convinced he has the most beautiful eyes I have ever seen—that's my baby.

March 17

I don't know why but I feel sluggish today. All I want to do is sleep. Jean and I chipped in and bought some pot. It sure was strong. I got high quick. When Jean and I left we met Frank and he turned us on with some pot. Afterwards, he bought me some coke. Boy!

March 18

Like Tom had told me before, he finally got the cocaine and he took me in the bathroom and let me freeze my tongue. He wouldn't give me much, tho, and he told me to never mess with the horse (heroin), for it wasn't any good.

March 19

Finally had that date with Larry, Jean was with Harry. They took us down to the Capitol and then to a Chinese restaurant. Larry kept getting on my nerves, for he kept kissing me on my neck and shoulder.

March 20

You know, diary, someone gave Tom some horse and it made him as sick as a dog. He was dizzy, etc. I walked all around in the street with him to try and clear his head. I even sat on the steps with him until daybreak. When I finally went upstairs he said he felt a little better. Don't tell me I'm getting back with him! I felt sorry for him tonight, tho. Oh, Mom didn't have the money for that job.

March 25

Daddy didn't come home until noon today. I don't know where the hell he was. Also you know, diary, something is wrong with Tom, for he had to go to the doctor's Monday for a shot of penicillin. I believe he has caught something. I certainly am glad I haven't been messing with him. Oh, yes, I didn't discover it until now but last night Tom took my locket off my neck (the one Steve gave me). I wrote a letter for Jean to give Tom about my locket but I forgot it. Tom came in (he gave me the locket). Tom is really something and I'm inclined to believe him more and more.

March 27

You know, diary, I must start going home early, for men are beginning to follow me home.

March 29

This morning Jean and I went to look for a job again with no luck. Tom wants me to quit Steve for him (I could hardly believe my ears).

March 30

I got up early today because Daddy came home drunk

with some of his friends. One of them got fresh with me, so I had to put him out. Daddy gave me money to buy a pair of shoes. They're real fine, too. Tom couldn't go to the show on account of his selling horse now. Again he asked me when I was going to write Steve. I just didn't answer him. He's so damn moody. I guess that's why I like him so.

March 31
After the dance, Tom took me uptown, bought some reefers and caught a cab.

April 3
I got up early this morning, for I couldn't sleep well for getting mad because I wasn't home yesterday when Steve called. I called Steve up. He sounded so nice over the phone that I almost forgot he was in California. After I got through talking to him who should call but Tom. He wanted to know who I was talking to for so long.

April 4
Every time I'm through with Tom something happens to change my mind. Well, last night I went and invited him to dinner. But he didn't show and Frank told me he had just gotten bagged. I only hoped that he didn't have any stuff on him. After a while, who should call but Tom. To tell the truth, I was very glad to hear from him. Tom was too smart to have anything on him.

April 8
Tom was cranky because he didn't feel well (horse again). He said he wished he could get Jill back again. I guess that's life though, when you have a good thing you always mess up. Well, I went home with Tom to get some more stuff. And if he wants Jill, he'll have to share her, I guess.

April 10

I dreamed about Tom last night. That kiss before he left sure upset me. I started calling Tom, but every place I called he had just left. About 11:30 he called. I told him to come up and he was here in less than five minutes. I enjoyed myself with him very much, except that he read one of Steve's letters that I had on my night table and I didn't appreciate that, because, after all, what Steve has to say to me does not concern Tom.

April 11

For some strange reason I didn't want to see Tom tonight. The gang had a dance and Tom went, but I didn't see him for I was with Eddie. Yes, diary, Eddie. Evidently Tom saw me, for he left, telling Jean to tell me to forget it. I couldn't care less.

April 12

I think the horse is getting Tom. He's so moody.

April 15

Dear Diary:

Tom is sick. I fixed the plaster for him—God only knows how I did—and gave him some spirit of niter for his fever, then I laid across his bed and went to sleep. I didn't leave until daybreak.

April 17

Both Harry and Jill called today. I said I didn't need money—anyway not that bad. Really!

April 21

Instead of going to White Plains we decided to get two sticks [marihuana] and a bottle of beer. It only gave us a buzz.

April 23
Tom wants me to write and tell Steve we're through
(now really, diary). I don't know how, but I manage to
avoid the issue.

April 25
I gave Tom money to get some C [cocaine]. It was the
money Mom gave me for the job. I wonder what's coming over me.

April 27
Tom picked up six sticks. Then we went ▓▓▓▓▓▓▓▓▓ We
were going to do them up in the show but some policemen were there. Tom smoked one in the bathroom. Well,
diary, when we got all lovey-dovey who should come in
but Jill. I don't know, diary, but I believe I'm actually
falling in love with Tom, although I honestly don't want
to, for I don't stand a chance and I know it.

April 29
Mom started a big argument with me. At first I didn't
pay her any mind but when she said I didn't go to a
party and I had been with Tom all night, I blew my fuse.

May 3
Tom bought some beer. We drank it and he gave me a
reefer. I smoked that and got a little buzz. Tonight he was
very sweet. Sometimes I almost wish there wasn't any Jill
between us. Because he is truly something wonderful and
I am very much attached to him. Don't know what to do
about Steve.

May 12
Mom said if I didn't get a job, she'll toss me out. She was
drunk, but I've got to do something because I need money
desperately. I'm worried about something. You know
what.

May 13

Tom has been avoiding me. I called and he didn't call back. They're all alike. That's what Jill said. She should know.

May 15

Finally saw Tom. He's the end. He acted like I was making it up. Honest, diary, I never felt so low. I feel like ending it all, but I don't have the courage.

May 18

████████████ Steve would like to end it as he's been hearing about Tom and others. He says his mother didn't write. I'll bet! Well, diary, Steve and Tom and the rest know what they can do.

May 20

I wish I could go to Mom, but I wouldn't dare. Daddy is no help. Called Jill and she said not to worry. She said Harry might help.

May 23

Dear diary, there's no other way. Harry said I needn't feel obligated, he was just a friend. I don't want to seem ungrateful, but where have I heard that before!

May 27

Tom is back, but I'm not interested. Guess his conscience is bothering him. Wrote Steve and told him it was okay with me. I've got other things to worry about. Saw Harry again. I'm scared, diary.

May 29

Told Mom I'd have a job soon.

June 29

Well, diary, it's all over now and I can breathe for the first time in weeks. I'll never make the same mistake again—I hope.

July 2

Called Tom and told him he didn't have to worry any more, just as though he had. He said I was a fool for not working for Harry. I hung up on him.

July 5

Guess I was a fool to believe Tom cared anything about me. He really had me fooled. It took a lot of stepping-on, but I finally know I don't belong.

July 10

I never felt this way before. All alone with nobody, really. I knew all the time that Steve couldn't work out. But it made me feel good to think about it. Sometimes I wish Mom would try to understand and help me, for I need a whole lot of help—but who wants to beg all the time?

July 12

Guess Tom was right, after all. You just got to help your-self. I remember once wanting to be a nurse, or else going to teaching school. I knew all along they were only dreams. I guess the only way you get anyplace is by hustling for it. I wonder whether I'll make a good hustler.

As I closed the diary, the detective's words echoed through my mind:

"We took down everything that mattered."

Exactly what *had* mattered? Thousands of girls were raised in homes like Peggy's without becoming prosti-tutes.

How significant was it that Peggy had turned from

Steve—the boy who loved her and who represented security—to a degenerate young dope-pusher?

Was the self-pity revealed in her diary a form of rationalization, gradually taking shape in her mind, for the decision she knew intuitively that she would make?

It was obvious that prostitution held a morbid fascination for her, it cropped up so persistently in the diary. She was indignant at being taken for a streetwalker, but not too indignant to record it as a constant reminder.

To what extent had narcotics contributed to her decline? I somehow suspected that this, too, was merely another manifestation of the disease that afflicted her.

I wondered whether Peggy would have the answers. Probably not, but I couldn't help wondering whether she had become one of the hundreds of prostitutes rounded up each year by the New York police.

CHAPTER 4

"Peggy got off as a first offender and hasn't been back—yet," the detective told me. "I checked the records for you."

"I wonder where she is now?"

The detective shrugged. He rose from his desk and went over to the window. "She's out there somewhere, loitering in halls, working the cheap bars, walking the streets. But we'll hear from her again. Her kind turns up sooner or later."

"Her kind?"

"Hell, yes," he said, "there's all kinds—just like there's all kinds of housewives or teachers or secretaries. Now if Peggy had been prettier—or brighter—she might have been a call or a pony girl."

"Pony girl" was new to me.

"You haven't been around," he said. "A pony is a cross between a B-girl and a call girl—I guess you know what they are. A pony's big-time stuff, but she picks her own men. They generally work out of some East Side bar where the Johns know how to find them. The bartenders freeze out servicemen and other stiffs because they aren't well heeled. The ponies are after big money. Besides, the girls say soldiers and sailors give them a hard time and try working their buddies into the same deal.

"Yeah," he added reflectively, "about the only people less welcome than servicemen are plainclothesmen. They never know for sure whether a strange John might be a cop getting ready to make a pinch—and I don't mean their arms!"

"Strange, this is the first I've heard about ponies," I said. "Where can I meet them?"

He grinned. "We don't run a date bureau."

But as I was leaving, he winked and said:

"Maybe some of these cab drivers could help you. They seem to get around."

That evening I telephoned a colleague who had an interest in adventure, and shortly before midnight we hailed a cab. I handed the driver a bill and said:

"Where's the action?"

"What kind of action?" he asked.

"Oh, the usual," my friend said, with a wink.

"Well, I know a lot of guys go to this one place," the cabby said. Then he hesitated. "But the girls coming out of there look pretty expensive to me."

"Drive on, James," said my friend.

We stopped in a seamy side street, near the East River, in front of a place that would have resembled a small candy store except that drawn curtains obscured the view from the street. It was squeezed between two warehouses, with fire escapes crawling down their exteriors. We would never have found it without a guide.

After being carefully scrutinized by a waiter, we were led to a nook directly across from the bar.

There were six or seven girls at nearby tables chatting among themselves and with the men at the bar. Two tables away, a blonde and a brunette sat together, toying with Martinis, and glancing at us frequently as they talked.

We overheard snatches of their conversation. The blonde was complaining that her last date had completely exhausted her. "You'd have thought," she groaned, "that this guy had never seen a woman before."

With that, a man at the bar laughed and called out

something to her. She stood up immediately and tossed her wrap over her shoulders.

"I don't think that's funny," she said, "but let's go."

The brunette, deserted, slid along the banquette and settled next to me. Clearly not more than twenty-two, her face was a smooth oval and her thick chestnut hair was combed back smoothly from her brow. She looked cool and chic in a black metallic gown which outlined her figure. Her voice was light and brittle and her remarks were punctuated with a charming laugh.

"No sense wasting time," she said pertly, "time is money. My name is Betty."

My friend ordered a Scotch-on-the-rocks for her.

"Everybody always asks the same questions, so I may as well save time," she announced, and proceeded to tell us the story of her life.

Betty came from Georgia, had been married at sixteen, was presently divorced, and had a child of three which she supported. "My marriage," she said indifferently, "never amounted to anything, the guy just wouldn't go to work. And so," she smiled, "I had to. Then I got pregnant, and I couldn't worry about him any more. I had Baby to think of."

She sipped her drink. "The baby has a maid, and we get along. Where else could I do as well?"

I picked up her drink and tasted it. It was little more than colored water.

"I could have told you it was water," she said. "What good would I be, drinking whisky all night?"

"Oh, he's one of these guys that like to know what he's paying for," my friend explained.

She seemed amused by the double meaning.

"About myself now," she continued brightly. "I suppose you want to know how I got into this."

She counted off on two fingers. "I do it for money—and for kicks. Sometimes I just like somebody, then I don't care whether he has anything."

"Do you like many of them?" I asked.

She glanced at me sharply. "As a matter of fact I do."

"That must be bad for business," my friend said cheerfully.

"Oh, no," she said. "Even the ones I like pay—it's just that if I liked somebody it wouldn't stop me if they didn't have money."

"I'll bet there aren't very many you like that much," he said.

"I don't know," she retorted, "I'm not so different. If I found the right guy I'd get married again. I'd even quit the business—except," she frowned, "if he couldn't support us the way I like. Maybe I'd keep on then."

We ordered another round. Betty raised her glass.

"My God," she spluttered, "they must have put whisky in it."

The waiter hurried over. "Anything wrong?" he asked. Betty looked at us. "Not yet," she said.

As the waiter retreated, her attitude became crisp and businesslike.

"If you're interested," she said, "and I assume you are, the waiter will check your credentials. If he says okay, I'll come along—provided we agree on terms."

"Let's have it," my friend said.

"First, do either of you have hotel rooms?" We shook our heads. "That's funny," she said, looking at us suspiciously, "practically everyone that comes in here is at some hotel. Nine out of ten, you know, are from out of town. I wonder what the New Yorkers do—they must go out of town for their kicks."

She sipped at her drink. "Anyway, there won't be trouble about a hotel. Some men," she explained, "are here with their wives, and get away just long enough to see us. We can't go with them, so we have to make arrangements. I can arrange the hotel. It all depends on what you want to pay—for a hotel, that is. I can get you a nice room in a good hotel near here for ten-fifty—that includes tax—or six thirty for a smaller room in a hotel that isn't quite as good."

"How about the room clerk?" my friend inquired.

"There'll be no questions asked," she said. "That has been arranged, too."

"What difference does the hotel make?" I asked.

She shrugged.

"It makes no difference to me. We wouldn't be there long enough for it to matter."

"Now about me," she went on. "I suppose you're wondering about that—I am fifty dollars an hour."

"Is that portal-to-portal?" my friend asked.

"Now that you mention it, yes," she laughed, "though I wouldn't fuss over a few minutes."

"Isn't that a little steep?"

"Perhaps," she said, "but look what you're getting."

"Would it be less for less?" my friend asked.

"By the time you get there and get out," she said shortly, "the hour is shot. I'm not used to haggling." Her eyes betrayed impatience as they shifted to the bar and then flicked around the room.

"I don't care much for hotels," my friend said.

"Well, suggest something." She leaned forward to face him directly. "Look," she said, "you don't know what you want, or maybe you do."

She stood up, curtsied mockingly, and flounced over to another table to sit next to a fat, bald man with a cigar who had just come in.

We paid the bill and rose to leave. Betty's head was averted as we passed, but her laugh rang out clearly. It didn't sound quite as charming as it had before.

We hailed another cab and left our destination to the discretion of the driver. He drove west to a shabby cross street off the Avenue of the Americas, two blocks south of Rockefeller Center.

From the street this bar looked little different from the other. But inside things were hopping. The girls were not as pretty or as expensive looking, but there were more of them and they were noisier. The men, on the other hand, were younger, not quite as well dressed, and kept to themselves. Waiters scurried around with trays.

The few servicemen at the bar appeared neglected, while the girls sat laughing and chatting together. Occasionally a girl approached one of the men at the bar but neither the men nor the girls seemed in a hurry to get anything started.

More girls arrived constantly, and were greeted warmly. A breezy brunette of perhaps twenty-three or twenty-four waved gaily to a young blonde as she strolled past her table. "Hi, Bertie," the blonde returned, "long time no see—where you been, on the Riviera?"

There was a chorus of good-natured laughter. "Been out of commission a while," Bertie responded with a broad wink. "But, boy, am I back!"

Several girls smiled brightly at us as we were shown to an aisle table. One of them, a tall slender brunette, paused at our table and playfully riffled her fingers through my friend's thinning locks.

"You're cute," she said.

He laughed. "My wife never tells me that any more."

"You been here before?" she asked.

We said we hadn't, but came recommended. My friend expressed interest in a yellow-haired girl with Dresden-blue eyes who was sitting alone in a booth. She didn't seem to go with the place.

"I'll try and get her," the brunette said, "She's a lovely girl."

We watched the two whispering together, but couldn't make out what they were saying. Both of them disappeared in the direction of the Ladies' Room.

When they came out, they sauntered over to our table.

"We're all prettied up now," the brunette announced.

The Dresden doll was even more beautiful at close

range. The brunette took the lead with a barrage of questions.

"Where do you come from?" she said.

"Tampa," my friend replied.

The brunette sniffed. "You don't look very tan to me."

"I try to keep out of the sun."

"What do you do?"

"Oh, I sell things."

"What hotel you staying at?"

"I'm staying with friends, in their apartment," he replied.

"How about you?" she said, turning to me.

"Same deal," I said.

The brunette looked at the blonde and said pointedly, "They're not staying at hotels."

"Why all the questions?" my friend said. "We haven't asked you any."

With that, she became friendlier. She told us that she was from Washington, had been in New York for only six months, and didn't want any trouble.

She said she was twenty-two but she looked older, and her Southern drawl was a little tired. There were deep circles under her eyes, and her lips curled down. Rested and relaxed, she might have been attractive.

Lowering her voice, she said:

"Maybe we can work things out somewhere around here." She turned to my companion. "It'll be thirty dollars, just for you, of course."

"Thirty *dollars!*" he exclaimed. "For what?"

The brunette smiled. "That's for you to find out."

Meanwhile, her colleague turned to me and whispered: "If that's too much, what can you afford?"

"It's not a question of what we can afford," my friend put in. "I just think it's out of line."

The brunette's good nature suddenly vanished. "What do you mean?" she asked coldly.

"I just don't think it's worth that kind of money," he persisted.

The brunette ignored him and focused her attention on me. She inspected me carefully, even peering under the table at my shoes.

"That's a pretty nice-looking suit you have there," she said. She fingered my lapel. "What did you do, change just before you came in here?"

"What do you mean?"

"You know," she said, "you look like PO-lice." She accented the first syllable as though it were the river in Italy.

"Why do you say that?" I asked.

"If you're not PO-lice," she demanded, "what are you?" I pointed to my thick-set, square-jawed friend. "I think he looks more like a cop."

"It's you I'm worried about," the brunette said. "I met a guy like you once, and was I sorry!"

The blonde who had been listening quietly spoke up unexpectedly. "The price," she announced, "has just gone up." She turned to me. "Have you got a thousand dollars?"

I didn't get it.

"Well," she said, "I think that's what I'd need for bail money if I went with you."

The brunette cut in. "How about seeing your credentials?" She looked at both of us. My friend laughed. "Now they want references—how about that?"

The brunette rose to leave. "You guys are all right," she said, "nothing personal, but I'm taking off. You're PO-lice."

The blonde seemed undecided, but when her friend gave a beckoning nod, she stood and said apologetically, "Sorry, but I think I'd better get going."

We left immediately and walked east. The evening had slipped away quickly, but there was still time. I had heard that there was a small night club not far away which featured a dancer famed for her beauty.

Actually, I had heard from an envious prostitute that the dancer was a call girl in flimsy disguise. She boasted that it cost $100 to get her phone number, $200 to take her to lunch, and $1,500 for weekend cruises. It was difficult to believe.

"Why does she bother with a night-club act?" my friend asked.

"That's easy," I laughed; "even Macy's has to advertise."

Then I added more seriously:

"She always knows what a guy it worth. She must carry a Dun and Bradstreet around in her head."

My friend laughed and said he would pick up a pseudonym for the occasion—a private banking house. "That's a name," he grinned, "that ought to impress her."

The club was like the others, with men and women three deep at the bar. Over the din of conversation and laughter we could hear the clang of a three-piece band that accompanied scantily clad girls, billed as performers, as they went through the motions of singing and dancing on a tiny square of floor.

As soon as a girl had finished her act she disappeared backstage for a few minutes and reappeared fully clothed at the bar. There she mingled with other performers and with the newly arrived men.

We bought a few drinks. The prices were steeper than those at the Stork Club or El Morocco. Most of the girls were ordering brandy. "We have to order that, or champagne," a buxom blonde singer told us. "It's the most expensive thing in the house."

The girl, who said she was from Buffalo, wanted to discuss literary matters when my friend told her I was a writer. She said she just loved Dylan Thomas. My friend had never heard of him. She eyed him contemptuously, but kept drinking our brandy.

All the girls at the bar had been in the floor show. We asked the singer if we could sit down with any of them.

"Sure, as long as they're our girls. No other kind are allowed in here anyway, unless they come with guys—and what guy would bring a girl in here?"

"How about later on?" my friend asked.

"What do you mean—later?" she retorted.

"You know what I mean."

She laughed. "The only thing we hustle here is drinks —I'd get canned if I took a live one out of here."

"How about the star?" my boy friend asked.

"Oh," the singer said, "I don't know about her. I guess she makes her own rules."

The star was just finishing her routine. It was an interesting, if not artistic, performance. We agreed that she was more remarkable for her beauty than for her talent. Besides a Grecian profile she had one of the best figures I had ever seen.

My friend motioned to a waiter and asked him to arrange a meeting. The man's face froze until they crossed palms. Then he led us to a table and disappeared backstage.

A few minutes later the star appeared and greeted us with a friendly smile. When my friend mentioned his name, I caught the quick interest in her eyes. She turned her attention to him and he appeared to respond.

"How about dinner some night?" he suggested.

She smiled. "Why not? But we'll have to get a few things straight, first."

"Such as what?" asked my friend.

She spoke casually, without a trace of self-consciousness. "Like what's in it for me."

My friend actually seemed embarrassed. "Don't you think that we should get together first and see how it goes?"

She looked at him with a glint of amusement. "I'll bet your family never made its money that way."

I was curious. "What are the damages?"

She ignored me, her eyes riveted on my friend.

"Yes, what are the damages?" he repeated.

As easily as if she were quoting the price of eggs, she said:

"One thousand for the night, five hundred for an hour or so."

There was a stunned silence.

She looked at us hard, curled her lips, and slid to her feet.

"Well," she said, "you know where you can find me."

As we passed the bar on our way out, the buxom blonde put a detaining hand on my friend's arm.

"Leaving so early?" she asked. "There's still a half hour to closing. After that," she winked mischievously, "I'm on my own—and we're not all stars."

CHAPTER 5

Back at headquarters, I had some questions to ask my friend the detective.

"I'd be greatly surprised," he said, "if any of the bars get a percentage of a girl's take. They're better off not even knowing, officially, what's cooking, so they can always play dumb if something goes wrong. It's really just a question of girls luring business into a place, before they lure it out."

"The pony girls seemed anxious to get moving," I pointed out.

"Without knowing the spot," he said, "I would still bet that there has to be some drinking before the girl leaves."

"Don't you think," I asked, "that some bartenders get kickbacks from the girls?"

"Maybe, but that would be a private deal. Unless I miss my guess, these bar owners aren't bothering with anything as obvious as kickbacks. The girls take the place of a floor show, and even when they happen to be out, the guys are still coming around and waiting for them. So they're still drinking. Figuring that the customer's whisky is cut, and the girl's is practically water, they do pretty good at a buck or a buck and a half a throw."

"What about the bar where the girl couldn't leave until the place closed?"

"That's different," he said. "On the books, the boss was paying her to sing, but her real job was hustling drinks. He'd probably get sore if he thought his girls were meeting guys later, because if a guy has fifty dollars to spend, he wants it spent in his place—on his booze."

"Off the record," I asked, "do you think there's such a thing as organized prostitution in this town?"

"Hell, no," he said. "A few pimps or madams may be operating with five or six girls, but that's the extent of it. This has never been a wicked city, in the sense of call houses or red-light districts."

"How about Polly Adler?" I asked.

"Even Polly Adler, in her heyday, was small potatoes. She had a house or two, but when the reform wave swept in they went out, along with a few others. Now, of course, you find girls hanging around bars and the big hotels, but for every professional you'll find ten amateurs. And it's no crime, so far as I know, for a man and a woman to start talking at a bar.

I still couldn't understand the need for procurers.

"Oh, there are reasons for it," he said, "but most of them are psychological. I don't get it myself. All I know is that a pimp is about the lowest thing around."

"I'd like to talk to one," I said, "but I can't get anybody to admit it."

He laughed. "It's certainly a dirty word, just like whore —they only call each other that when they play rough."

He thought for a minute. "There's a pimp I know that you might find interesting. He's a real character. He's out of business now, so I don't think he'd plead the Fifth."

"Retiring on the profits?"

"Hardly. We call him Willie the Weasel, and when you see him you'll know why. No, poor Willie was a hophead, and his money went for dope. He had seven or eight girls at his peak, I understand, and between the dope and trying to please the girls he's pretty beat up."

"And how does our friend Willie get by?" I asked.

"Oh, he picks up a few dollars here and there, peddling information. He hears things once in a while, but mostly he's in and out of Riker's Island, trying to kick-off the dope. He says he's off the stuff, but I've never met one yet who could keep away."

The detective wasted no time. I received a call from him the next day setting up the appointment. I was to meet Willie in a downtown restaurant, where we could sit for hours without being disturbed.

"How'll I recognize him?" I asked.

"Just remember the name," the detective said, "and you can't miss him."

Willie was sipping a cup of tea when I walked in. I spotted him immediately. He was slight to the point of emaciation, his frail shoulders stooped, and the skin was taut across his bony hands—he looked exactly like a weasel.

But it was his face that gave him his name. It was small and wizened, like a prune, and slanted down from knobby cheekbones to a narrow pointed chin. Wisps of hair poked out of his large drooping ears and his slit of a mouth revealed two irregular rows of yellow teeth.

His voice was a low, rasping whine, very like that of a whipped cur. As he talked, his fragile body was racked with spasms of coughing. "From smoking," he said. "I should stop, but it's all I got left." He managed a little smile, but it was more of a leer.

I would have imagined him to be at least sixty, but he told me he was forty-nine. He had been procuring since he was fourteen, until his "retirement" five years before. At the pinnacle of his long career Willie had managed a household of five girls, in which, by self-proclamation, he was supreme.

"But I never made a prostitute or a dope addict," Willie said hoarsely. "You have to believe me. I never made one of those girls do anything they didn't want to. They were all hustling somewhere, in the dance halls or on the streets, when I found them, and"—his squinty eyes lit up

—"nearly every one of them came to me by their own choice."

Willie wanted it established from the beginning that he was no pimp.

Pressing a hand to his heart, he said with a grimace, "It hurts me right here when a girl gets mad and calls me a pimp. It's real ingratitude."

He held out his hands, palms up, in a gesture of helplessness. "How can they say I'm a pimp? I don't drive around in no Cadillac. It's a partnership. They do their share and I do mine."

"What did you do, Willie?"

"What do *I* do?" He ticked off his functions on tobacco-stained fingers.

"When they got arrested, I went down and saw that they got bail. When they needed dope, I saw that they had a fix, if I had to go out and boost a store for it. When a John gave them a hard time, I'd go after him with a bat."

Willie slanted a smile at me. "Because I'm small, people think they can push me around. Well, I wouldn't take nothing from nobody—those Johns knew better than to cut up around my place. Sure, I took the money, but I gave back for it. If I couldn't make a dollar in a nice way, I wouldn't do it. I never mistreated a girl—I don't care what they said. When I beat them sometimes, it was for their own good."

He crossed his arms over his heart. "Believe me," he said, "I always tried to be considerate. I'd never whip a girl in front of anybody else."

"Why did you have to beat them at all?"

Another spasm overtook him, and I waited patiently for him to recover.

His voice was almost a squeal now. "You don't understand," he said. "You've got to teach them a lesson, or they have no respect. They're not like other people. You can't trust them." He leaned over and spit on the floor.

"You can't trust them no farther than that. Now you take Patsy. She was a good girl, the best girl I had, but she was crazy like the rest of them. She was always getting drunk on the job. No stability. Losing her money or giving it away. I gave her a couple of warnings, but she wouldn't listen."

He held up his hand. "Believe me," he said, "I may die on the spot, but I always gave warning. And I'd always wait for the right time and place, if I had to teach them. This one night, when Patsy came in drunk with nothing in her pocketbook, I took her in a room and locked the door, then I took off my belt. She cried, but if I let her get away with it, the other girls wouldn't have no respect. It wasn't just for me, it was for all of us."

I must have looked puzzled.

"You don't understand," he said; "we all needed the money—it was for all of us, not just me."

Drugs were a constant problem for Willie. With six addicts in the house, including himself, it was a perpetual drain on his pocket—and ingenuity. And the girls were not always as generous as he.

"Whenever I had the dope," he said, "I'd give it to the girls. Believe me, I never held back. But not them." His voice became scornful. "You couldn't trust any of them. There was once I couldn't get the stuff anywhere. The only ones that had it were the drugstores and they wouldn't give it out without a prescription. One day I went to thirty-three drugstores and they all turned me down."

Willie reached under the table and held up his feet, "I wore my shoes out, walking for those girls," he whined, "but I couldn't get anything—no heroin or morphine or even demerol."

Tears actually came to his eyes. "So I got home very tired and discouraged, feeling very jumpy and all, and needing a fix pretty bad.

"On the way in, I noticed this doctor's car in front of the house."

Willie tapped a finger against a sunken temple. "Now, I get to thinking, after I get in the house, that it's kind of odd, because the doc is in with Patsy and she hadn't been sick—they'd always tell me when they were sick. But I decided, what the hell, the doc is like all the other Johns."

My face must have registered surprise.

"Sure," wheezed Willie, "the doc was a John. We didn't have to pay him. After he made a call, he'd just see one of the girls. Anyway, when he came out of Patsy's room, I grabbed him by the arm and said, 'Gee whiz, doc, haven't you got a couple of pills for me— even demerol?' "

Willie broke off to explain. "That's a synthetic. We call them demmies. If you can't buy H or M, why, demmies will do the trick."

"But how about the doc?" I asked.

"Oh, yeah, the doc," Willie said, with a smile that made him look more like a weasel than ever. "The doc just laughed and says to me, 'Willie, you know I can't pass that stuff out—not even to the girls.'

"You know how you get a feeling somebody's lying. All of a sudden it come to me. While I'd been getting more nervous every day, Patsy grew calmer and calmer. Then I remembered how she smiled when I complained about not getting a fix for so long. I didn't say anything to the doc, but as soon as he got downstairs, I went into Patsy's room. 'Where is it?' I said. She was sitting on the bed. 'Where's what?' she said. I took her by the wrist and smacked her hard across the face. 'Don't lie to me or I'll tear you apart. Where is it?' I was younger and stronger in those days, but I could still show them right now if they got fresh."

He leaned back, apparently satisfied that I was impressed with his strength.

"What did the girl say then?" I prompted.

"She got mad and called me a pimp." He looked at me with an injured expression.

"She shouldn't have done that," he said sadly. "So I let her have it, what else could I do? I didn't like to hit her like that, but what can you do when they make you?"

Patsy had staggered to the dresser, pushed it aside, and pried a small tin from a crack in the floor molding. Inside the tin were six tablets—the balance of the demmies she had been getting from the doctor.

"Imagine," Willie exclaimed almost reverently, "the thinking that girl had to do. I always said she was the smartest of the girls. But I had to teach her a lesson. So I took all the tablets away. If she hadn't been so selfish, I would have shared them with her. I always shared with all the girls."

"How many did you give the other girls?"

Willie hesitated. "Well," he said slowly, "you see, there wasn't enough for all the girls and I didn't want to play favorites."

"So you just kept them for yourself."

"Well, if you want to put it that way."

Willie complained of feeling tired. We ordered more hot tea, and it seemed to revive him.

"There's one thing you got to understand," he said, "it was no easy life with those girls. And those Johns"—he sneered—"they didn't make life easier for me, either. You had to watch them all the time, but you can't be every place at once. I must of been in one of the rooms when this guy came in, drunk. One of the girls had picked him up in a bar. She shouldn't have done it without knowing something about him. So when I come into the room, this drunk looks at me and says to the girl, 'Get that little pimp out of here or I'll throw him down the stairs.'"

Willie laughed like a weasel. "*He* throw *me* down the stairs—humph. He shouldn't have said that, because I never did anything to him. But I kept my temper. I just told him to speak nice or get out. So he calls me this again, and I run into the room and get the bat."

Willie laughed until he began choking again. Tears were streaming down his face. "He was a big John, believe me, but by the time I worked him over with the bat, he was glad to fall down the stairs and get out of there. You should have seen him run into the street holding on to his pants."

little peephole in all the rooms and I could watch them all from my room—just so," he assured me quickly, "that I would know what was going on. I used to have to hold on to my sides, or I might have split a gut from laughing. They were a howl. Some of these old guys with the big bellies would stand there and say to the girl, 'Whip me.' So she'd whip, until they were screaming. And they'd scream, 'Harder, harder!' And you should have seen the looks on their faces—like baboons." He snorted. "And then they'd go back to their wives, or maybe their offices, and I bet everybody would treat them with respect, believe me."

Willie never knew when an emergency might arise. "One day," he recalled, "one of our regular Johns—a big lawyer—got so excited that he started choking one of the girls. He didn't know what he was doing. If I wasn't looking through the peephole she might have been dead. So I go rushing in, but I can't pull him away. So I get out the bat and rap him a couple and out he goes. Believe me, I didn't like to do it, but I couldn't let him strangle the girl, could I? You should have heard her gasping."

He rattled his throat to show me how bad she was.

"How about the man?"

"Well," he said, "when he didn't come to, I started to worry. So I got a bucket of cold water and threw it on him. He started to move and I got him down to the street and told him not to come back."

"Was that the last you saw of him?"

"No," said Willie, "he was a real degenerate. One night I looked out a window and I saw him sitting on a fire escape outside one of the girls' rooms. He was getting kicks out of watching." Willie cackled. "I threw a dish at him. You should have seen him scat."

were making for me," he complained. "They had everything a girl could want—money, clothes, good times, rich Johns, and they'd sit around crying and wishing they were dead. It was enough to drive a man nuts, believe me."

He shook his head. "They just don't have any consideration, these girls. They'll do anything to make a man miserable."

Every one of his girls had tried to end her life, but Willie was too quick for them. One night he was almost put out of business by a suicide pact.

"When I got home, all of my girls was unconscious. Two were curled up in a bed; the three others were sprawled over chairs and on the floor. I could smell the gas. The windows were all shut and the jets were open. It was smothering, and the girls weren't hardly breathing. I had to do some fast thinking. I threw up the window, closed the jets, and then ran down to the drugstore and called an ambulance. Then I called the cops, because I figured the police emergency squad was what I needed. I hung up quick before anybody asked questions. Then I kept away from the apartment until the girls were back from the hospital and the cops had finished up."

There were other emergencies, equally challenging. "Another time," he said, "this girl took an overdose of heroin, and it put me in a hell of a spot, believe me. I wanted to save her—she wasn't a bad kid, only inconsiderate. I knew the intern on the ambulance wouldn't know what she'd taken, anyway not in time to do any good. Once you go into a coma, it's curtains. So I rushed to a booth and called the cops. I told them to tell the ambulance doctor what antidote to bring and then I hung up fast, so they wouldn't waste time."

Willie's eyes brimmed with nostalgia. "I saved that girl's life, but do you think she was grateful? Not her. She left me the first chance she got." Then he added savagely: "She started listening to one of these madams, and the first thing I knew she was working for her."

Willie, having spent his hatred, sank back in the booth. I felt an overwhelming desire to hear no more about prostitutes that day. He agreed to come to my office the following day. He was there when I arrived.

Although the office was warm, Willie refused to remove his overcoat. The coat was bigger than he was. His hands were lost somewhere in the vastness of its sleeves, and he could hardly stand erect under the weight of it. Willie himself weighed barely a hundred pounds.

He had no trouble remembering where we had left off. "These madams got no honor," he said. "They'll do anything to take a girl away from you. They fill her head with all kinds of promises, but about the only thing they do for her is take her money."

"It doesn't add up, Willie."

His voice rose. "Don't you see, they got ways of getting closer to these girls than a man has."

When I remained silent, he added impatiently, "They're all degenerates, every one of them."

"But, Willie," I insisted, "they must do something."

"Listen, boy," he said, "these madams make big promises, but I delivered the goods."

"What kind of promises?"

The question seemed to annoy him, and when he got

excited or annoyed his speech became blurred and his grammar deteriorated.

"Oh," he said, "they tell them lots of things, like what they'd do for them when they're sick or broke, or when the cops give them a hard time. But," he snorted, "they don't do nothing. They send them out on all kinds of jobs, without even knowing the John. All they want is the money."

I was intrigued. "Well, you took all their money."

"Sure, but I spent it on them. That's different."

"Sure," I said, "and you beat them, too."

"You don't understand. That's what they wanted." His little weasel face twisted into a grin. "That's why they did things they shouldn't."

"Yes," I said, "I've heard that masochism is common among prostitutes."

"I know what that means," he said proudly, "and all women are like that."

He leaned across the desk, poking a bony finger at me. "It's all an act," he wheezed, "but they never fooled me. When I was younger I used to go to my sister's house. Her married girl friends were always complaining how tired their husbands were. I knew what they wanted. They were all ready. Later we'd sit around and smoke and laugh and they'd say what saps their husbands were. And they were right—a husband's like a pimp, the woman's got him working for her."

Willie's distaste for women went back to his boyhood in Italy, when at the age of twelve he had his first experience with a prostitute.

"It was just after the first war," he told me, "and all the prostitues had jammed into Milan. I was staying with an uncle. He didn't care what I did as long as I kept out of his way. So I got to hanging out with these girls. They liked me around, like a sort of mascot, and I'd run their errands for them. They hardly ever left their rooms, because they might be picked up, so I brought in the business.

"They'd send me around to the railroad station and the cafés to tell young English and American officers where to go for a good time. After the officers were gone, the girls would fool around with me.

"There were three or four girls in a room, but they had curtains between their beds. One day a girl took me behind the curtain and showed me. I remember how she laughed. And the worse I felt the more she laughed. I didn't know then what she was doing, but I knew it wasn't right.

"Believe me, I didn't know what it was all about until I was fourteen, and then something happened to me. They all laughed about how I was a man now and that they didn't have to teach me no more. It was like a big joke, and I got to laughing about it myself, so nobody would know it bothered me.

"By the time I was fifteen I could teach some of them a few tricks, and they didn't laugh no more, believe me, not when I was around. That's when I learned you have to be tough to get respect—and don't ever trust them, or you'll be sorry.

"They used to fight a lot. I stopped that, too. I became like a referee. Believe me, I couldn't stand it when they were screaming and tearing each other's hair. That's when I had to start using a whip. I didn't want to, believe me, but they made me."

Willie had been born in America, but his Italian-born parents had taken him back to Italy. They had been killed in the war. When he was seventeen and already a dope addict, he returned to the United States.

"It was easy to get the stuff over there," he said. "The medical corps all had plenty, and the soldiers used to pass it out or we'd steal it. The dope makes everything wonderful at first. You're not afraid of anything, you think you can jump over a mountain or be like Toscanini." He smiled. "But you can't."

Dramatically he peeled off his overcoat and then his jacket, rolled up his shirt sleeves and showed me an emaciated arm in which the veins were collapsed. "From the needle," he said. "I got no more veins."

Then his dull eyes brightened. "I don't fool with it any more. I kicked it off."

"So you're cured," I said.

He nodded. "It took some will power, I can tell you."

"Did a doctor help you?" I asked.

He hesitated. "The cops picked me up for dope, and the judge said he'd let me off if I went to Lexington—that's the government hospital for addicts in Kentucky.

"That was okay," he said, "but," tapping his head, "here's where they got to cure you—upstairs."

Even at Lexington, Willie was on the alert for a fair prospect. All it required was patience, enterprise, timing —and a knowledge of women.

"I spotted her one day across a room," Willie said. "She was about twenty-eight and a looker. There were guards all over the place, but I got a note through, and she got one back. There was separate quarters and all that, but there was ways of sending notes in the laundry. I told her I'd be waiting for her when she got out."

"How did you know she was a prostitute?"

He looked at me as though I were an idiot.

"She was on the dope," he said.

"She was a good girl," Willie went on, "a high school graduate, too, and seemed willing. I showed her how we could make a thousand a week following the harvests. We'd get a car and travel through the wheat fields of Kansas and Dakota, when the men were getting paid off and didn't care about money, or make the beet season in Colorado and Utah, and then on to the West Coast for the winter, where we'd take the easy picking at the tracks. Then in the spring we'd go up to Alaska for the salmon catch. It was all set, and we couldn't miss. But she took to drinking, and pretty soon I couldn't talk to her. Then she went back on dope, and it didn't do any good trying to beat any sense in her. I finally had to give up in Cincinnati, before we got started, and I went back to New York alone."

I asked Willie if he had ever worked at anything. "Sure," he said. "I worked the tracks all the time. I'd go up and stand next to the best-looking girl, like I was with her, making sure some of these guys saw me. Then later I'd go over to one of these jokers and tell him I could fix him up if he'd make a bet for me."

"You mean something like that worked?"

"Hell," Willie said, "how many times have they sold the Brooklyn Bridge?" What began as a laugh ended in another coughing spasm. "Wouldn't those dames have been surprised if any of those guys came over!"

Willie also worked at picking pockets, shoplifting, and pimping, which he considered the most demanding work of all.

"It was all in picking the girls," he said. "You had to be careful or they might get you in a jam taking goofballs, and winding up in Bellevue, or rolling some John who'd run to the cops. I always told my girls to play it straight. You did just as good that way, and didn't take chances. Sometimes you even did better, like the time that Patsy—the smart one—brought back this ship's captain with her. Any girl but Patsy, and I'd have gotten sore. I didn't like drunks around. But Patsy was a cool one, she didn't drink on the job and she made no mistakes. The captain had $1,800 in cash with him. When he started drinking, another girl might have tried to roll him. But not little Patsy. She gave him a hard-luck story. You know, like she was going to have a baby and what was she going to do."

Willie's eyes gleamed. "That Patsy sure knew how to pour it on. All evening she cried and said how could she have fun with this on her mind. The captain said all right, how about a couple of hundred? Patsy laughed and said he must be captain of a small ship. That got the captain mad, and he said how it was the biggest damn ship on the line. Finally, he brought out his wad and started peeling the bills off. When he put $800 down on the bar, Patsy picked up the money and piled into a cab with him. We stayed up drinking for a while and Patsy and I took him to his boat at eight o'clock. He wanted to show us how big it was. We had to laugh all the way back to the house. It was watching all those men salute the captain as he marched up the gangplank in all his dignity and gold braid, especially," Willie laughed, "when I got to thinking how he looked through the peephole."

Willie has no respect for marriage. Once a detective said to him, "Willie, how can a fellow like you be a pimp?" Willie returned angrily, "You're a pimp, too. You keep a wife." Other detectives intervened to save him from a beating, but Willie only grinned complacently.

When Patsy announced after eight years that she was retiring to get married, he could hardly believe it. "I don't know why she did it, believe me," he said. "It almost broke my heart. I always treated her good. She didn't give me warning. She said she was tired and wanted a home of her own, but I knew she just wanted to hurt me —that's how they are. She was over thirty and not so pretty any more. If I was one of those madams, I'd have kicked her out a long time ago, but I always took care of the girls. I knew it wouldn't work out, but she was a long time finding out."

After Patsy left, some of Willie's other girls began talking marriage. "There was this one girl," Willie said, "who put the idea in Patsy's head. She was no good. She wound up in the bughouse after taking some pills." His eyes brightened. "Guess what? She got friendly with one of the guards and they got married after she came out. I wonder who was crazy."

Willie had other personnel problems. When careless or drunk, his girls frequently became pregnant. "This one case," he said, "was bad because she waited too long and couldn't have an abortion. But it was her own fault, she drank too much.

"It was a nice baby, but it looked Oriental, and that's how we knew who the father was. It looked like this guy who used to come around and take her dancing." He shook his head. "She was a funny dame, she said it made her feel like a kid again to go dancing. This guy wanted to marry her, but Aggie wouldn't think of it. Her old man would have killed her if she married an Oriental. He thought she was in a Broadway dance hall, and he didn't like that. Anyway, things worked out because the baby only lived ten days. But I never saw anything like that girl. She kept holding the baby in her arms and crying. She wouldn't even give it to the undertaker, but the doc finally gave her something that put her to sleep. She wanted to bury the baby next to her mother in the family plot in Jersey. But we talked her out of it. If her father found out he'd have killed her, and me too.

"We all went over for the services. We hired a big limousine, for all the girls, and the kid was buried in the same cemetery, but a different plot. It ruined Aggie. She couldn't eat, sleep, or work. I tried to get her to take a few jobs, thinking she'd forget, but she just kept staring out the window. Even when I got her a fix she wasn't interested. I finally had to get rid of her. Believe me when I say it hurt me. But she cut her wrists one day, then she took sleeping pills. The other girls were upset all the time and nothing got done.

"After that," said Willie, "I drew the line on Orientals. They caused me too much trouble. So that left us only with white, because the girls decided for themselves they wouldn't take Negroes. Besides, a lot of Johns won't go with girls that don't draw the color line. They don't care what the Supreme Court says about this segregation business. And you know something? Some of these girls are a lot fussier than those Park Avenue dames—they just won't do everything, believe me."

In the old days Willie had recruited most of his girls from Broadway dance halls. "Look," he said, "I never made anyone do anything they weren't already doing. All these girls were working in these dance halls, selling tickets, just so they could meet guys for later. Hell, some of these joints just had a phonograph—and it wouldn't have mattered if it wasn't working. The best any of them got was twenty bucks for the night, and they never knew what they might run into. You didn't have to talk them into it, because they could see how much better off they would be, and they wouldn't have to stand around and dance with a lot of jerks."

The dope habit, affecting Willie's health, was eventually his undoing. "I couldn't hold on to the girls the way I used to. I'd keep getting sick all the time, from getting the dope or not getting it, and the girls took advantage. When I got sick, they'd just go wild. They didn't remember all I'd done for them. So I decided I'd only have a couple of girls, maybe only one if she was reliable. I settled on this little Southern girl. She had a nice drawl and didn't look like she'd been around. I knew she was on the stuff, but I thought I could handle her—we could take our shots together. But she didn't have no discipline. She'd leave the things around, so if anybody came in they could see the needle and the bent spoon and the rest. Then she'd mess up on her dates, and the Johns would get sore."

Willie's reedy voice became a whine. "Hell," he said, "I used to go out and hit all the bars for her, and come back holding the John by the hand."

He held out his hands expressively. "What did *she* have to do—I ask you?"

"The trouble with the dope," Willie said thoughtfully,

"is that when a girl's an addict, she won't go out on a job unless she's had a shot right before. Once she's hooked, she couldn't care less about sex, believe me. But when she's off the stuff a while, all the sex that's been lying there dormant in her begins to wake up and she starts to react to a man's touch."

Willie chuckled. "Boy, you ought to see them when they get like that. They go all their lives and don't feel anything for a man, and then this thing happens to them. They need a shot right away, believe me, or they'd die just thinking of what's happening."

Again his voice rose, and he looked at me with his little weasel eyes. "You see," he said, "that's the things I used to do for them. I'd keep the stuff around, so they wouldn't have to worry about not having it.

"But believe me—" Willie solemnly held up his hand— "I never started a girl on the dope. I wouldn't want that on my conscience, believe me. I was always nice to my girls."

CHAPTER 6

Days later I sat in Women's Court watching a dreary procession of streetwalkers parade before the embarrassed magistrates of the City of New York. Some of them might have been Willie's graduates.

I had received permission to visit this court, which is normally barred to spectators, and was allowed to sit on a bench next to the presiding magistrate.

There were only a handful of people in the courtroom —lawyers, witnesses, and defendants. Prostitutes were whisked in and out of back doors. Bailiffs guarded the entrances and others patrolled the courtrooms. The prostitutes themselves seemed too dazed and uncertain to care what was going on around them. Their fight had been lost long before they reached Women's Court.

They were of all ages and descriptions. I saw a pregnant girl of seventeen sent off to a penal farm to receive prenatal care and escape the procurer who waited for her outside. I saw an old hag of fifty or more, so dirty and disheveled that I wondered how any man could possibly have found her attractive. I saw women sobbing in fright and anger, in a drama of degradation that even the seasoned magistrate sat through uncomfortably. At one point he turned to me in exasperation: "I don't know why they keep bringing in some of these women. What am I supposed to do with them? How does it help to throw them in jail? They pick up worse sex habits there, and then go back to the street. Besides—" he shrugged—"what have they done that the man hasn't? It takes two to commit this crime."

The magistrates appeared to make every effort to give common streetwalkers a chance. They examined the police and other prosecution witnesses closely, suspending sentences when they were forced to convict.

"I give them every break I can," one magistrate told me. "If there's no record of a recent arrest, drugs, or venereal disease, I'll generally give a girl an SS—if there isn't a pimp in the background. But I'm not sending any of these girls back to those jackals if I can help it.

"Three-fourths of the prostitutes in Women's Court have resorted to drugs—many indoctrinated by procurers who are well aware that an addict will do anything to get money for dope."

It was difficult for me to distinguish the addicts from the others. Most of the prostitutes in Women's Court looked as if they had been put through a wringer. One of the few exceptions, an attractive teen-ager, had been introduced to drugs by a classmate at school. The first few shots were free, until she became addicted, and then it became expensive.

"I couldn't think of anything but dope," she said, "and needed fifteen to twenty dollars a day for it. Where else could I get it? I didn't bother with boys. They didn't have money. I had only done some necking before, but when I needed a shot I'd do anything for it, though I felt less like sex then than any time."

She had been arrested for soliciting and admitted that she had smiled at men in the street and in shops and restaurants. They always smiled back, she said; it was not hard to imagine the rest.

The scarecrow of fifty was called up before the bench. Her corded arms hung limp at her sides, and she could hardly keep her eyes on the magistrate.

"Have you an attorney?" he asked.

She didn't seem to understand. He repeated the question. She shook her head. The magistrate nodded to a young lawyer from the Legal Aid Society, which represents more than 50 per cent of the prostitutes haled into Women's Court, and then gently pursued his questioning.

"When was the last time you were here? Now tell the truth and maybe we can help you."

The defendant looked dazed. She pushed the stringy hair back from her eyes.

The court stenographer repeated the question.

"Fourteen years ago," she mumbled at last.

The magistrate turned to me. "Fourteen years," he whispered. "She's doing better than we are."

The prosecution called two witnesses, the arresting officer and the customer. The officer, young and eager, testified that he had watched the woman approach three men in the midtown hotel area. Only one stopped and talked to her. A few minutes later the officer trailed her to a public telephone and overheard her make an appointment.

"She asked this man if he wanted to have a party," the officer said; "then I heard her say she would come up right away.

"She repeated his room number on the phone. I gave them a few minutes and then went to the hotel. I knocked on the door. He didn't answer right away. When I entered the room I saw the man, partly dressed. I went into the bathroom. She was putting on her clothes. I opened her purse. There were three new five-dollar bills in it, with consecutive serial numbers. The man had admitted giving her fifteen dollars."

The judge leaned toward me and whispered: "You can't blame these cops for doing their jobs—besides, they're young and want to get on."

The officer continued: "I asked her where she got the money. She denied he gave it to her. But after I told her what he had said, she admitted it."

The magistrate interrupted him sharply.

"You know better than that," he told the officer. "I'm not supposed to know she admitted anything. After all, she says she's not guilty. I only want to know what you saw."

The prosecution's principal witness was the man in whose room the woman had been arrested. He corroborated the officer's testimony in an all but inaudible voice.

The magistrate turned on this middle-aged buyer from Ohio, who was squirming uneasily on the stand. Abruptly, as though he were the counsel for the defense, the magistrate took up the questioning.

"Speak up," he commanded shortly; "this is not the place to be bashful. We want to hear what you have to say."

The witness cleared his throat. "I was walking along when she came up to me and asked me if I was interested in a party."

"And what did you say?" the judge inquired.

He shifted uncomfortably.

"Nothing definite," he said.

"Well, did you encourage her interest?" the magistrate persisted.

"Not exactly," the witness replied.

"Well, did you discourage it?"

The witness hesitated: "I didn't encourage her and I didn't discourage her."

"But you gave her your number, didn't you?" the judge rejoined. "That means it was all right with you—doesn't it?"

The man kept looking at his shoes.

"Well, doesn't it?" the judge proceeded impatiently.

As the witness nodded, the magistrate dismissed him curtly. But as he was leaving the stand the magistrate said:

"One more question. Are you married?"

The witness wet his lips nervously.

"Speak up," the judge snapped.

"Yes, sir," the man replied.

He left the stand, and the magistrate turned to me. "I asked him that on account of her. He just admitted adultery, since he's married, and he comes in and testifies against her. Adultery's an offense, too, but all we do is hold the woman. It's not fair, but what can we do?"

The defendant again faced the judge, awaiting his verdict. Her face was devoid of expression and even her eyes looked dead. Only her lips moved but no sound emerged.

The judge's voice was gentle.

"I'm going to have to find you guilty," he said. Then he turned to a court attendant and, pronouncing each word clearly, he said, "When you bring her back tomorrow, I'll suspend sentence."

Still in a daze, she was led away for overnight detention.

"Normally," the magistrate confided to me, "I don't tip a sentence, but I didn't want to keep her in suspense."

To my surprise, I found that even when the male is the aggressor, the law finds only the woman guilty.

This point was developed dramatically at the trial of a 23-year-old Negress accused of soliciting a 35-year-old white man near Rockefeller Center.

A large florid attorney, counsel for the defense, contended that his client should be acquitted since the man had actually started the conversation.

The man visiting from New Jersey, had emerged from Radio City Music Hall at about midnight. He had walked only a short distance when he was face to face with a young girl strolling in the opposing direction.

Both had paused.

"What are you doing?" he asked.

"Nothing," the girl replied.

"How'd you like to do something?"

"All right."

By an unwritten code that seems to guide such meetings, each miraculously understood the other.

"Do you have a hotel room?" the girl had inquired.

The man shook his head. The girl mentioned a hotel where no questions would be asked.

They discussed terms in the cab.

"She wanted fifteen dollars," the man testified. "I didn't have any change, so I gave her two tens and told her to keep them."

Meanwhile, two crusing plainclothesmen had observed the incident and trailed them to a cheap hotel, where the man signed the register and paid for the room. After allowing time for them to disrobe, the policemen entered the room. The woman was arrested and the man detained.

Reluctantly, the male witness described the meeting in the street. The defense attorney pounced triumphantly on his admission of making the first overture.

The magistrate whispered scornfully: "He's just playing for the grandstand. The girl thinks he's doing a great job for her, but he knows the law as well as I do—he's here oftener than I am."

The judge rapped his gavel. "Look, counselor," he said, "let me get a word or two in edgewise. A higher court ruled that it doesn't matter who makes the first move, the man or the woman. So long as the girl responds, she's the offending party. The law is clear on this point—so there's not much sense discussing it."

I heard frequent charges of frame-up by prostitutes who had been trapped by plainclothesmen posing as customers. The magistrate pointed out to me, however, that this was almost a routine attempt to win judicial sympathy, confuse the issue, or get back at the arresting officer.

"The police aren't angels," the magistrate admitted. "But why should any cop want to frame these girls—most of them don't have the money to pay a lawyer."

He laughed grimly. "If there were a payoff, it's a cinch the case wouldn't get to court."

Although magistrates privately denounce police entrapments, they accept it as a penalty for keeping antiquated antiprostitution statutes on the books and the only way of keeping prostitutes off the streets.

"After all," the magistrate remarked, "you do have to keep these women out of sight, for appearance's sake if nothing else. It seems a hypocritical attitude, but it's the only practical one. Otherwise our streets would be overrun."

He sighed: "We sweep the dirt under the rug and hope nobody will look for it."

I observed with interest the demeanor of plainclothesmen accused of frame-ups. While not ruffled or disturbed, they smiled self-consciously, obviously aware that they did not cut a gallant figure.

Through a Spanish-speaking interpreter, hard pressed to keep pace with her, a short, swarthy woman protested that she had been tricked by a policeman as she rested on the fender of a car parked in the street in front of her apartment building. The time was 1:30 A.M.

"What were you doing in the street at that hour?" the magistrate asked drily.

She fanned the air furiously with her hand. "Hot," she said, "very hot, trying to get air."

The magistrate looked unconvinced, and she broke into a barrage of Spanish. The interpreter translated in a monotone: "By all that is sacred, on the heads of my two children, I swear I had nothing to do with this man."

The woman appeared to be in her late twenties.

"You have children?" the magistrate asked. "How old are they?"

The woman smiled and held up her fingers. "Three and five years."

"Then why," he asked, "weren't you at home with your children?"

The explanation came gushing out: "I was in the street only a few minutes, just getting a breath—" she gasped—

"when he come over and say it's hot and wouldn't I have a drink with him."

She admitted joining the officer at a nearby tavern and going to a hotel around the corner. As she testified, she glanced contemptuously at the apple-cheeked young officer, a man of about thirty.

"I don't know what I do," she said, "because he give me so many beers and I get dizzy." The translator added blankly: "She says that she wasn't used to drinking, and besides the heat made her woozy."

The prosecuting attorney turned to the interpreter. "Ask her how many beers."

The woman hesitated, then held up three fingers. "Three beers."

"They must have been large beers," commented the judge.

The interpreter repeated his comment in Spanish.

"Yes," she agreed quickly. "Large beers. Besides, I'm not used to drink."

"Yes, I know," the judge said, "all you do is take care of your children, whom you leave alone while you sit around in the street, and go off to a saloon and a hotel with a strange man."

When the officer testified that she had agreed to go with him for $5, she cried out and had to be held down in her chair.

"He lie. Big lie."

The judge warned sternly against demonstrations. ███████████ silently as the arrest was described. The officer, prohibited by regulation from removing strategic clothing, had opened his jacket. As the woman disrobed, he identified himself and told her to get dressed. She tried to escape, but was overpowered after a brief struggle.

The judge found the woman guilty. He shook his head as she was led off, sobbing.

"I think," he said wearily, "we'll call it a day."

CHAPTER 7

Looking at Jane it was hard to believe that she had ever been a defendant in Women's Court. In fact, it would have been hard to believe that she was a prostitute at all had she not been telling me so for the past hour. Jane was a beautiful girl, with a sophisticated sense of humor, and seemed to enjoy talking about herself. Nevertheless, I was rather surprised that she mentioned her arrest voluntarily.

We were in the living room of her apartment near Central Park. She sat in a large wing chair, facing me across a marble-topped coffee table. The subject of marriage came up, and she told me that she had been maried twice and was thinking about it again but couldn't quite make up her mind.

The young man in question, who as yet had no inkling of her profession, had been urging her to marry him. Meanwhile, he had been taking up a large part of her time, causing a drastic reduction in Jane's usual income, from $1,000 a week to an occasional $100 or $200.

"Are you in love with him?" I asked.

My question apparently amused her, for she laughed and said, with a roll of her blonde head, ████████ who knows about love?"

"But you must know something about marriage," I insisted.

"You can say that again," she replied. "But maybe I was just unlucky."

"Is he in love with you?"

She grimaced. "He says he is, but how can you tell? If he finds out I'm a pros, that would end it. I'm pretty comfortable here," she said. "I'm not crazy about giving it up."

"Then why bother?" I asked.

At twenty-four or twenty-five, she was possibly at her professional peak. She drank very little and shuddered when I asked if she used drugs.

And, although she said she smoked only on her dates, I noticed that she virtually chain-smoked during our interview.

"You seem nervous," I remarked.

She hesitated for a moment, and then decided, apparently, to make a clean breast of it. I sensed a need in her to tell someone.

"Frankly," she said, " the boy friend isn't my only reason for cutting down. I guess I could have done all right when he was busy or out of town."

Absently, she patted the little Pekingese that had jumped into her lap. Practically every call girl I met owned a dog or cat. Jane was unusual only because, in addition to the dog, she kept a pair of love birds.

"There's somebody," she said finally, "who's out to get me—a cop. I'm scared stiff of him. He won't quit until he gets something on me."

She shivered, as though chilled by a sudden draft.

"I never want to be in that court again. They treated me like I was a streetwalker. And all the time I had the feeling this cop was enjoying it. I don't know why, but he goes after all call girls. Maybe some girl gave him a hard time and he's getting even. Another girl informed about me. She was jealous, I guess, or trying to talk herself off a spot.

"Anyway, he came to the apartment one day and warned me that if I kept on he'd get me. He had blue eyes and they seemed to be laughing at me. I told one of my girl friends about it and she said it looked like he wanted to get paid off. But if she had seen him she'd have known better. He got his kicks out of catching people like me.

Anyway, I got all upset and talked it over with a few Johns. They told me to get myself a new phone number under another name.

"I tried meeting all my customers outside. But one day this fellow stopped in without warning. Before I let him in I looked down the hall, and didn't see a soul. We were sitting around when the cops almost knocked the door in. There were three of them in the doorway, including the one who was out to get me.

"They couldn't budge me, so they went after the John, but he kept denying everything, too. They must have been a long time at the door, because they repeated our conversation. Then the John had to admit we'd been together, but he said he hadn't paid for it. After all, what we had done was our business if I didn't get paid for it.

"They picked up two hundred-dollar bills which the John had left on the table. But he said we were old friends and he was just paying back a loan.

"They started bullying him, telling him they'd run him in, too, but he stuck to his story."

Jane shuddered as she recalled her day in court. "It was a nightmare," she said, "being treated like a prostitute, seeing all those dirty old hags and wondering if I'd ever wind up that way.

"I was afraid it would get in the newspapers and then everybody would know—I would have died if my mother found out. I kept thinking they might even have photographers there but, thank God, I wasn't important enough.

"One of my Johns got a lawyer for me. He was a lawyer himself, but I guess he didn't want the cops asking him questions.

"But what saved me was the John. He kept sticking to his story. I could see the judge getting impatient. He told the cops: " 'If this man said he didn't give the girl any money, what are you bothering me for? You know you don't have a case.'

"Then the prosecutor started to say something, and the judge cut him off. He said, 'This case smells; I'm throwing it out.'

"I was beginning to breathe again and then he motioned for me to stand up. I could feel my knees knocking together. I was sure he could see right through me. He looked me in the eye. I tried to look back, but couldn't make it. He spoke slowly: 'I don't want to see you in here again. If I do, you're going to jail.'"

In the corridor outside the courtroom, the plainclothesman had stopped her. "You haven't seen the last of me," and he smiled.

"It started me thinking about giving it up, for a while anyway," she said, "but I didn't have enough saved up." She circled the room with her arm. "It's all here," she said, "and on my back."

But she had already begun to curtail her activities when she first met The Boy—as she called him—at a gathering of showpeople, businessmen, socialites, playboys—known collectively as café society.

"This older man, about sixty, said he would give me $50 just to go there with him, and that after the party I could go off with somebody else. I had to promise I wouldn't tell anybody I was a pros." She laughed. "He didn't have to worry."

While she stood chatting with two girls, The Boy came up and introduced himself. "I didn't pay much attention to him," she said, "but he kept following me around the room, asking for a date. I finally decided I'd have nothing to lose, since I might be out of business pretty soon anyway.

"He was a nice-looking fellow, from a good family. Right away, he was talking about his mother and how he wanted me to meet her. He sent me so many flowers the place smelled like a funeral parlor. Pretty soon he was coming over every night, and I didn't have time for anybody else. He'd just sit around and ask questions. He kept wanting to know where the money came from and all that. I told him everything, except what I was doing. I said I modeled for a living, and I had, as a matter of fact."

"He can't be very bright," I ventured, curious to see if she would spring to his defense.

"I don't know," she shrugged, "maybe he loved me."

While we were talking, a beautiful redhead, slim but sensuous in a sleeveless maroon sweater, strolled casually into the apartment, removed the dog from Jane's lap and carried it off without a word. Only as she was leaving the room did I notice that she wore ballet slippers.

Catching my look, Jane laughed. "That's my girl friend Marge. She lives across the hall. She thought you were a John and didn't want to get in the way. It's lunchtime for little Peke."

"Any more in the building?" I asked.

She answered with good grace. "Oh, no, this is a very respectable building. They think we're models. Marge has a way of just coming in, but I walk in on her, too. One day she barged in while The Boy was sitting around. We hadn't expected him. There were two other girls and six Johns waiting over at Marge's. They were getting impatient, but what could I do with The Boy here. I kept saying I had a headache, but he wouldn't go.

"Marge was in such a rush that she didn't see The Boy until it was too late. She yelled, 'Jerry and the others are getting edgy. You better get moving.' I could see The Boy looking at us, but it meant $200 and I needed the money. Besides, I was getting tired of his snooping. I pushed him out the door, kissed him good night, and said I'd tell him about it the next day.

"The first call the following morning was from him. He said I had some explaining to do. I said it was just a date with a friend of Marge's. When he wouldn't buy that, I told him I got paid for going out, and that's why I had to leave."

"And that convinced him?" I asked.

"Well, I didn't say what I got paid for. If he'd only known"—she smiled ruefully—"that two of those guys were for me."

Jane had other plans, which did not involve prostitution —or matrimony. She was studying singing and dancing at her suitor's expense and was aiming at a career on stage or television.

"They tell me," she said, "that I have more versatility than a lot of those dames on TV."

We both laughed heartily. Then I asked Jane if she would mind talking about her marriages.

"They weren't much," she said. "I was only sixteen, the first time. I wanted to get away. My father was one of the biggest Johns in town. He finally left us. We tried to get Mother to divorce him and find some happiness, but she buried herself in religion. She went to church every day and expected me to go with her. It was too much for me.

"I was going out with this boy in the neighborhood. He was three years older than I and unhappy about his family, too. Anyway, we finally eloped. His family was Jewish and they didn't like it any more than mine. As a matter of fact, my father got so upset he even came home to see us."

Jane soon had to admit that her family had been right. Within a few weeks she and her husband had to appeal to his mother for living expenses.

"He wouldn't work," Jane said. "He was a regular psycho. He kept saying he was mentally disturbed, and he finally convinced me. He was physically disturbed, too, and it was starting to give me a complex. But one day we were sitting in a car, with a friend of his, when he started telling the friend what a great figure I had. For a while I didn't get it. I thought he was only trying to build me up, but when he tried it again, on somebody else, it suddenly dawned on me what he was up to.

"I don't think he was doing it for money. I guess he

just figured it for kicks, but he was always complaining that his allowance was cut off because he married me. So I don't know."

The marriage was annulled after three months. Jane returned to her mother and attended secretarial school. But boredom overtook her and she decided to marry again, this time a man of her own faith.

"This was even more comical than the first," she said. "I left an idiot to marry a madman. In three years there wasn't a day we didn't have a fight. He'd have a fit if I went to a movie with my mother. When I'd get home, he'd twist my arm until I said I had been with a man. I'd ask him to call my mother, but he'd scream that she was in it with me.

"When he was drinking he'd beat me for having been to bed with another man. He never considered I'd been married before—it was adultery as far as he was concerned, because I hadn't been married in the church."

I was curious as to how she broke away.

"I tricked him," she said. "One night after I had been with some girls, he started to accuse me of the usual thing. He kept screaming at me to confess the truth. Finally, I said, 'All right, I cheated—I've always cheated.'

"He stood there petrified, and I ran out before he had a chance to recover. The next day I called and said I was getting a divorce. He said he'd always known I was a whore, and it couldn't be too soon for him."

She caught my unspoken question.

"It was all a lie, of course, there weren't any others. I was about six weeks pregnant and knew I was stuck if I stayed. He didn't know or he would have come after me."

"And the child?" I asked.

She shook her head. There was no regret in her. "It was born dead. That sort of simplified things. I don't know what I would have done if it had lived."

I still didn't know how and why Jane had turned to prostitution. She discussed it frankly.

"I got a job modeling in the garment district. It was one of those jobs where you modeled in the showroom and typed letters for the boss. I made a fast fifty a week at first, but I was prettier than the other girls and caught the boss's eye. He said he liked the way I moved. One night he asked me to dinner. I knew he was married, but if he didn't care, why should I?

"Nothing happened the first few times." She laughed. "You know what I mean, but he gave me fifty anyway. Then we started having a relationship. I didn't have the feeling I was getting paid for it, since he had given me money before just for sitting around. Besides, he was nicer than the men I had been married to. He'd give me fifty, sometimes a hundred, depending on how he felt. I got more in one night than I made all week modeling.

"He must have told his partner about me, because the partner invited me out, too. He said it was all right with my boss. It didn't make me feel any different. I felt the same at the end of the evening as before. They gave me the money because they liked me."

It was through another model that Jane expanded her activities. "One day," she recalled, "I was having lunch with this other girl. She wore a dress that cost two hundred and she'd just bought a Cadillac convertible. I thought she must have a generous boss, but she laughed and said:

" 'I couldn't do it on fifty a night, believe me. I go out with buyers with fat expense accounts. They don't get in town often and they really appreciate a girl. Why don't you say something to your boss? He'll help a girl like you.' "

That night Jane visited the girl's apartment and was impressed with her Louis XIV dining room, her 27-inch television set, her closets crammed with Fifth Avenue labels.

"I gave it some careful thought," Jane said, "and decided to join the club. So the next morning I went to my boss and said I'd like to go out with some of the buyers. He said: 'Why not? You're a nice kid, and you've earned a break.' "

"In two weeks I quit modeling. I was getting a hundred most of the time now—never less than fifty."

From a small furnished room on New York's unfashionable West Side, Jane moved to the desirable East Side. As a precaution against seasonal slumps, she purchased the telephone numbers of well-known Johns from procurers and madams, exchanging others with call-girl friends.

She enjoyed her new way of life. "I liked going to smart supper clubs. I liked paying $100 for a dress instead of five. I liked dating men who were rich and successful, instead of kids who were all hands. I liked the way headwaiters bowed and scraped in clubs where I couldn't have gotten past the front door by myself. Like everything else, it's great if you're successful."

"You must meet some interesting people," I said.

She shrugged. "There's not much to remember. They're like any other girl's dates, except that I can always predict what's going to happen. How many girls can do that?

"Generally," she said, "I'd go to the customer's apartment or his hotel room, but we'd go out to dinner first or a cocktail party."

However, there was always something to worry about. Besides the threat of arrest, there were the usual occupational hazards of pregnancy, venereal disease, and exposure. "To stay around," she said, "you have to watch yourself like an athlete. I'm examined by my doctor once a week. Sometimes he'd give me antibiotics to be on the safe side, but I try being careful, even though my customers are the careful kind, too. As for pregnancy, I don't want that ever again. Besides the discomfort, it puts a girl out of circulation."

Exposure was possible without arrest, and equally painful. "I always look around a room fast when I go to parties," she said. "You never know. Once I ran smack into two of my cousins. They were with a couple of call girls and didn't even nod to me. I took my cue—hoping they were too busy thinking of themselves to wonder about me. I always wondered what I would do if I ran into my father, since he was around quite a bit. One night I opened a door and there he was standing right in front of me, talking to a young redhead. He was laughing and had his hand on her shoulder. I turned around and ran out before he could see me. I wanted to throw up."

For the first time since the interview began Jane rose from her chair. She walked over to a little cart and mixed herself a horse's neck. She asked if I would care for a drink. "I keep about everything for the guests," she said, in a flat voice. Then she looked at her watch. It had been a long interview. "I've got to go, but if you have any more questions, get in touch."

As I was leaving, she suddenly remembered something. "Stan," she said, mentioning the publicity man who had arranged the meeting, "said you did features about entertainers and people in TV."

I nodded.

"Well, how about a story on me? I've been on one show already."

"I'll speak to Stan about it," I said.

The following day I telephoned Stan.

"Hell," he said, "I had to tell her something or she wouldn't have talked to you. I'm handling her publicity, you know. She's been getting write-ups in all the columns —under another name. And she's beginning to believe them."

"How many names does she have?"

He laughed. "Three that I know of—the one she started with, the Oldest Profession name, and her newest professional one."

Long after I left Jane I kept thinking about her. I wondered whether she would marry The Boy, although I was almost certain she was not in love with him or with anyone else, but was toying with the idea of marriage only to keep an avenue open should other things fail.

Since I didn't know her new name, I had no way of knowing how she was doing in television. It was also possible that with time she would lose her fear of the police and go back to being a full-time call girl.

When this book was going to press, I telephoned her. She recognized my name at once and seemed friendly.

"Are you married yet?" I asked.

She laughed. "Not quite."

"Still afraid he'll find out?"

I could hear her amused chuckle. "Hell, no," she said, "he's already found out, and loves me more than ever."

"How did he find out?" I said. "He seemed so trusting."

"It was some of the girls," she said. "They went to him and told him I was a pros."

I found this genuinely puzzling. "Why would they do that?"

"Oh, I don't know," she answered. "I guess they were mad because I had a guy that wanted to marry me."

"They must have liked you," I said.

"Oh, let's not talk about that." She sounded annoyed.

"So then what happened?"

"Oh, he came over and made a big fuss and wanted to know if it was true. I suddenly got tired of it all and told him if he couldn't take me as I am, the hell with it."

She was laughing.

"What's the matter?"

"I was just thinking about it. Boy, did I get mad. I asked him if he was a cop, or something, always snooping around. Frankly, I was glad it happened. I was tired of hanging up when the phone rang just because he was around, and I was tired of losing money.

"When I got all through, I figured that was it. Instead, he tells me that he loves me and wants to marry me right away. He said he was willing to forgive and forget, so long as I didn't do it again.

"He said he'd give me a hundred and fifty a week to live on until we got married, if I wouldn't see any of my old friends or"—she chuckled—"make any new ones."

"Did you keep your promise?"

"In a way," she said. "Well, I didn't see how it would hurt if I saw two or three old friends a week, just for dinner or a couple of drinks."

"You mean they were satisfied with just that?"

"Most of the time," she said. "You see, they're married, and live in Brooklyn, or Long Island, and have to get home—so they're gone by the time he gets through work. As a matter of fact," she said, "that was the nicest thing that ever happened to me—finding out that I had friends who wanted to help me. And all I had to do was explain the situation—they couldn't have been nicer."

"But when are you getting married?" I persisted.

"Well, I want to see what I can do with acting first. I've explained to him that if we were married and had a fight, he'd throw it up to me. He said no, but that's the way men are." Something else struck her. "Hell," she said, "my last husband threw it at me when I wasn't even doing it.

"Another thing, I told him everybody was bound to find out sooner or later, and then he'd start to suffer and wind up making me suffer."

"What was his answer to that?"

"He said nobody had to know. We'd buy a house in the suburbs and keep to ourselves." She laughed. "Half the people I know come from the suburbs."

Against her better judgment, The Boy had finally persuaded her to meet his parents. "He wouldn't take no for an answer," she said. "We went to this fancy party on New Year's Eve at a Fifth Avenue hotel. There were lots of people milling around. I looked them over while The Boy searched around for his mother and father. It must have cost them a few thousand for the champagne and whisky alone. Everybody was drinking like there was no tomorrow.

"They seemed nice, but I could tell right way that his mother didn't like me. She was too polite. His father looked like one of my Johns. He had a nice round face, without much in it, a few wisps of gray hair, and a shiny head. I could almost see him getting ready to pinch me as I turned around. We had never met but I could see him trying to remember me. I was a type he was used to. As I kept looking around the room, I saw a dozen Johns I knew. They were with their wives and I could tell they were worried. I let them worry."

Some comment seemed indicated. "It certainly was a Happy New Year's."

"Yeah, it wasn't a bad party, but it started me thinking. It was bound to come out sooner or later, and I didn't want any more kicking around. I told The Boy he must be pretty mixed up to want to marry somebody like me. I even asked a psychiatrist about it. He said The Boy was trying to play hero subconsciously—everything is subconscious with those headshrinkers—and was really building up his own ego by being the great martyr."

"How do things stand now?" I asked.

I could almost see the expression on her face as she said, "Well, I just can't see putting all my eggs in one basket—can you?"

CHAPTER 8

"Have you ever heard of a thousand-dollar call girl?" I asked the Inspector.

"I told you nothing would surprise me."

However, he agreed that the dancing girl whose performance I had seen the night we toured the bars was clearly exceptional. She was unique not only for her beauty and her rates, but for the grand manner in which she operated.

But, unlike other prostitutes, call girls often dabble at other jobs, drifting into prostitution after brief modeling or television careers, and frequently mingling with people who have no idea that they are prostitutes.

In their leisure hours they try to improve themselves, brushing up on current events, the theater, and kindred arts. Many are glib conversationalists, repeating parrot-like what they have heard and read.

"They read a book review," the Inspector remarked, "and then they tell you all about the book."

Because their dates are by appointment only, they run less risk of exposure than prostitutes who solicit in bars and on the streets.

Ordinarily, call girls prefer older—and wealthier—men because they demand less and pay more. "The younger ones," one call girl commented, "want to make everything a great romance—and then talk as though they made a conquest."

Call girls are the solace of tired businessmen who, oddly enough, are never too tired to seek the company of a young woman. "Some of these girls are so beautiful and impressive," the Inspector observed, "that the older John is proud just to show them off."

By not establishing a price in advance, many call girls earn even more. "Let the Johns think you like them for themselves," a girl said, "and there's no telling how they'll spread themselves. Sometimes they put five hundred in an envelope and call it cab fare. The sight of their own money seems to embarrass them."

It is not difficult to become a call girl. Procurers haunt bus stations, airports, and train depots, eager to assist wide-eyed innocents or designing newcomers. Despair, loneliness, and the mirage of glamour help do the rest.

Many call girls are only too happy to sell or give away the telephone numbers of the wealthy Johns who have been the cornerstones of their own careers.

"These numbers," the Inspector told me, "change hands faster than a Virginia reel, and the Johns never complain."

Because they integrate themselves with a social pattern, call girls do not come to police attention as often as their less fortunate sisters of the night. "How can you find them?" the Inspector asked. "They're almost part of the decorations at some of these café society spots."

Occasionally, however, there is a special reason for rounding them up. Once the notorious Jelke case broke, the State was determined to obtain a conviction against socialite Minot (Mickey) Jelke on a procuring charge. A dozen call girls whose names had been mentioned over tapped telephone wires were promptly subpoenaed as witnesses, presenting a spectacle police and the public will long remember.

When the shock of arrest had worn off, a few of the girls even tried to tempt their captors. "There was no respect in them," the Inspector said, "either for the law or for the men behind the law."

One of the most glittering beauties housed at city expense during the Jelke trial was soon attempting to corrupt the only man in sight—a plainclothesman standing guard outside the door of her hotel room. "She did a slow strip tease," the Inspector said, "trying to make him forget he was a cop."

He shook his head. "These girls are just too much for me."

Suddenly, as if an idea had struck him, he began to riffle through the pile of papers on his desk, and in a few seconds he triumphantly waved a copy of a summons before my nose.

"Remember the call girls I told you about—the two that looked so terrific I couldn't believe my eyes?"

I nodded. "You were going to let me know when their cases came up."

"Well," he said, "you can see them for yourself. They'll be in court later today."

He reviewed the case briefly. Wire-tapped conversations had enabled police to arrest the two girls in the Park Avenue hotel suite occupied jointly by several businessmen from Detroit. "I hardly think," the Inspector commented, "that these boys will be around for the party today."

The madam who had arranged the party had been arrested at her home. Recalling the arrest, the Inspector grinned. "She was so mad she walloped the cops with her pocketbook. You know, I've been after her for seventeen years. But she might beat it yet."

Women's Court is not far from Police Headquarters, and I arrived with time to spare. There was the usual bustle in the courtroom. A clerk informed me that the only witnesses were the arresting officers.

No one was surprised by the conspicuous absence of the businessmen in question. "They'd be crazy to show up," an attendant said. "They're prominent enough to get in the papers."

I spotted the two call girls at once. They sat in the front row, a blonde and a brunette, one on either side of the madam, looking singularly out of place in contrast with the procession of unsightly slatterns I had seen on my first visit to this courtroom.

Both were unusually attractive. Barely beyond their teens, they were slim and well formed. Their dark, loose-fitting suits looked expensive enough to carry Hattie Carnegie's label. Their faces, however, showed strain, which was accentuated by an absence of make-up. They sat rigid, intently watching everything going on around them.

Occasionally they turned to the madam, but she continued to stare directly ahead. She was a large, buxom woman who could easily have been mistaken for the headmistress of a school for girls.

Her face was round and puffy, its pallor emphasized by a heavy veil of powder. Her unblinking green eyes were fastened on the magistrate. Conscious of her scrutiny, he finally whispered to me, "I'll bet they'd never guess her on 'What's My Line?'"

The first witness, a young and rather handsome policeman, was called. He was identified as the officer who had transcribed the wire-tapped conversations and later participated in the arrest. In a singsong voice, he read from his shorthand notes. When he described specifically how the madam's phone had been tapped, her eyes froze and her square jaw tightened.

Fleetingly, she shifted her gaze from the bench to a middle-aged woman in black. In the middle of almost every sentence, this tiny birdlike woman would get to her feet and lodge an objection. She was counsel for the defense.

The magistrate leaned toward me and remarked, "That madam hates men so much she wouldn't have one for a lawyer." He shrugged. "But this woman's not a bad lawyer. It's just that every time she's in here, you get the idea she's fighting a cause. And maybe she is."

The officer, his shorthand prowess challenged by the defense, was now outlining the educational background

that qualified him to testify. Again the defense attorney
broke in, while the prosecutor groaned and the magistrate looked annoyed.

"Your honor," she said, "this man is obviously not a
stenographer. I move for dismissal."

The prosecutor, a dark man with a look of infinite
boredom, answered testily:

"We're not saying he's an expert. We're only saying
that he jotted down what he heard, and that there's nothing wrong with either his hearing or his shorthand for
the purposes of this trial."

The sarcasm was lost on the defense counsel. She faced
the judge with determination.

"Your Honor," she declared, "I question whether this
young officer could accurately follow the conversation
he is reading back. I do not question his good intent,
only his ability to recapture the conversations."

She requested and was granted permission to dictate
two or three sentences to the officer, which he was then
to transcribe and read aloud. As she dictated, the officer's
pen flew over his pad. He looked flustered. "Nobody
could keep up with that," the prosecutor objected.

The magistrate nodded. "It does seem a little fast."

"That's my normal talking voice," the woman attorney
rejoined.

The prosecutor was amused. "We won't question that,"
he grinned, "but the girls speak slower—they have to be
understood."

Having at last transcribed his notes, the officer was in-
structed to read them to the court. The defense attorney
interrupted several times to point out the discrepancies.
However, she was compelled to agree that the transcrip-
tion was substantially correct.

"I think," the magistrate said, "that we can now get
on with the testimony."

One of the girls followed the legal maneuvering with
dull, vapid eyes, while the other looked defiantly around

the courtroom. She successfully stared down anyone meeting her gaze. The hostility in her was almost electric.

When the young officer continued to read from his notes, however, both trained their eyes on him. His testimony was terse and to the point. Reporting that a male voice had opened the first tapped conversation, the witness turned to the magistrate. "Shall I identify the voice?" he asked.

The magistrate ruled that the name wasn't relevant. "As I understand it," he said, "you're just trying to show here how the whole thing worked." The prosecutor nodded.

The testimony continued.

"Hello there," the unidentified male declared.

"Hi, Stan," the madam replied.

"How about tonight?"

"Who do you want?"

"Sandra."

"Okay. Where?"

"The lobby of the Hotel ——, at the cigar counter."

"No three-hour deal now, Stan."

"Okay. I have to be out at nine-fifty, anyway."

"Okay, Sandra, at seven P.M., at the cigar counter. You know how much?"

"Right. Goodbye now."

The madam made a telephone call. A woman's voice responded drowsily. It was three in the afternoon.

"Hello, Sandra dear," the madam said. "I got an important message for you. Got a pencil and paper? Now write this down. Seven o'clock tonight. Hotel ——. Cigar counter.

"He told me he'd give you fifty and no three hours. His name is Stan."

"Does he know what I look like?"

"I told him dark hair, blue eyes, and tall. He knows you. Good luck."

The magistrate turned to the witness. "Was anybody arrested in that case?"

"No, sir. We kept watching the line."

"Then why bring in these conversations?"

The prosecuting attorney stepped forward. "We are trying to show the pattern of operating. Now we're ready to develop the case itself."

The witness fumbled through a sheaf of notes and looked toward the bench. "Shall I begin now?" The magistrate nodded.

The next transcribed call was from a call girl identified only as Patty. For some unexplained reason, she had not been summoned as either a defendant or a witness.

The witness continued reading as though quoting stockmarket reports.

"How are you, doll? This is Patty."

"So-so," the madam replied.

"I have something for you," Patty went on. "A friend of mine, Gus, is in town. He's in the lumber business. Whenever he gets in town he wants somebody—usually a hundred or more. If he doesn't like a girl right away, he'll give her something and send her away. If he likes her, she gets one hundred or more. We're going to meet him later. In the meantime he wants some company. I don't know who to ask for. This is a guy you'll like a lot. He's a big fellow and he drinks a lot, but he's a spender."

"What time, honey?" asked the madam.

"At apartment F, the —— hotel, at seven o'clock tonight."

"Okay then. Where is he from?"

"Detroit."

"Detroit!" she repeated. "That's the cheapest bunch."

"Not this guy," Patty said. "Not Gus. He usually gives a hundred or more. And if he doesn't like a girl, as I told you, he gives her something anyway. Sometimes, too, he sees the same girl two or three times."

"Is that all for the evening, doll?" the madam inquired.

"I don't know," said Patty, "but I think you ought to know that Gus likes blondes."

"I'm expecting to hear from Mary," the madam returned. "She's a blonde."

"Fine, even if he doesn't like her, he'll give her something. Gus is a great guy."

After hanging up, the madam had some calls to make. The first was to Sandra.

As the witness pronounced Sandra's name, the girl's eyes smoldered. She whispered something to the madam, who shook her head without looking at her.

Both leaned forward as the witness resumed.

"Listen, Sandra," the madam was quoted as saying. "Here's the address. Now write that down. This is a fine man. He's terrific. He's a right guy and will give you something regardless."

"What's his name?" Sandra asked.

"Oh, I forgot."

As the witness paused, several people in the courtroom laughed. The madam glared, Sandra looked sheepish, and the other girl maintained her vacant stare.

The witness droned on, still reading. The two women, he reported, said goodbye, and before the madam could make another call, her telephone rang. It was Mary announcing that she was calling from the airport. She had just arrived and was checking in.

Briefly, the madam repeated what she had told Sandra.

"Are you interested?" she asked.

"Sounds like fun."

"Get there as soon as you can," the madam said. "Sandra will be there, too. She's a lot of fun and she plays the accordion."

Even the witness looked puzzled. I wondered whether the reference to an accordion had cryptic significance or whether it meant precisely what it said. I never did find out.

The witness concluded his testimony. Under further

questioning, he stated that he had accompanied the raiding party that arrested Mary and Sandra. Patty had not yet arrived at the hotel suite.

Because the other members of the raiding party were not in the courtroom, the trial was adjourned.

The madam, flanked by her girls, left the court. Evidently, they had had no difficulty in raising bail.

There were several postponements of the case. Several weeks later, I telephoned one of the clerks at Women's Court to inquire about subsequent developments.

"Oh, that case," he said. "Yeah, I remember that one on account of the girls—real beauties. Yeah, dismissed for lack of evidence."

"Oh, yes," I recalled, "they couldn't get the boys friends in to testify."

"Hell," he said, "they couldn't even get in some of the cops."

CHAPTER 9

I was sitting in an East Side bar, talking to the bartender, when Georgia sauntered in. She walked by without a word, settled at a small table, powdered her face, and ordered a Martini.

The bartender, whom I had given $10, told me that she came there every day at five o'clock.

When he led me to her table, he whispered, "Better not say you're a newspaperman. I didn't tell her that."

She looked up coolly. "This is the fellow I was telling you about," the bartender said lamely. "He just wants to sit around and talk to you. You can trust him."

She motioned me to a chair.

Georgia was no beauty, but she had a bold, compelling eye. She studied me quite candidly as I ordered a drink and said evenly:

"You're not a John."

I nodded.

There was little inflection in her voice, and her eyes wandered as she talked.

I had been told that she was an articulate girl, once married, who had an interesting story. She was about twenty-six or twenty-seven, and her skin was still fresh. "It'll be a couple of years," I thought to myself, "before she curls up." There was neither hostility nor welcome in her attitude, only watchfulness.

I felt that frankness would be best. "I'm a reporter," I told her, "looking for a story. The story happens to be prostitution."

Her expression remained the same.

"As you probably know," I continued, "very few girls understand how they got into prostitution in the first place, and fewer can express themselves."

I told her that the bartender had remarked about her intelligence. "He said you were different from most of the girls."

At last she began to thaw. "Oh, I don't know about that. Maybe I've had more to think about." She finished her drink. "What kind of things do you want to know?"

"Oh, anything that comes to mind—how you got started, what you feel and think."

She still didn't trust me.

"How do I know," she asked, "that you won't mention my name? I never saw you before."

"Your name," I said, "is meaningless in this case. I don't even have to know it."

She promptly told me what it was. Then she said that she could not talk with me for long since there were a few phone calls to make, which meant she would have to be on her way depending on what transpired over the phone.

"I don't like to use the phone in the apartment," she said, "it might be tapped. So I usually start out from here, take a couple of drinks to wake me up, and then get going."

"Have you ever been arrested?" I asked.

"No," she returned, with her first flash of spirit, "nor do I intend to be."

"If you can help me," I said finally, "there's no reason why I shouldn't pay you for your time."

She snorted. "That won't be necessary. If I say anything, it's because I have something to say."

I sipped my drink and waited. It was obvious that coaxing would accomplish nothing. I talked about the theater, literature, television, and she joined in, almost as though we were on a date.

As we were both laughing at a stale joke I had dredged

up, she said, "Go ahead, ask me a few questions. How can it hurt?"

Generally I opened these interviews with a few stock questions—how long she had been in the business, how she happened to be in it at all, what she thought of it, where she thought she was going, and where she had come from. That seemed to cover the situation, since all conceivable details could be developed from these points.

I asked Georgia how long she had been a call girl.

"Oh, about two years," she replied, "maybe three. I get a little hazy about it sometimes. Things get blurred."

She needed more encouragement.

"You know," I said, "many of the girls have difficulty in recalling their experiences—I suppose it's because the men are pretty much alike. Does anything in particular stand out in your mind?"

"They all stand out," she said.

"But some must stand out more than the rest," I persisted.

"I'll never forget my first date," she said. "It was enough to discourage any girl. It was a nightmare."

Most of the girls I talked to had vivid remembrances of their first professional engagements. It seemed only natural. But Georgia's was special.

"Mine was really something to remember," she said. "It was enough to make you give up. It'll never happen again, that I'm sure. I wouldn't take anybody under forty for a million dollars—even if they put it in escrow."

I made no comment.

"That was a night I'll never forget. Do you want to hear about it?"

"Very much," I said, "but not if it will upset you."

She replied disdainfully:

"The man doesn't live that can bother me that much."

I listened attentively as she began the story:

"I had just come up from Florida and was living with this other girl, who was a friend of a guy I knew. She was about thirty-five, but was getting too old for parties.

"I stayed with her until I worked up a clientele of my own. She gave me a list—people who are in the papers all the time—and all I had to do was mention her name when I called. She was to get twenty dollars a name and I was to pay her off as I went along.

"I was a little nervous about meeting new people, but she said everybody would treat me like a lady.

"My first job was a bachelor party, at a Park Avenue hotel. She said I should get twenty to thirty dollars from each guy, or whatever I could get, since it was a sort of package deal.

"She laughed and said it would be fun, since they were young and full of pep. It wouldn't take long."

I asked how much her friend was to get.

The interruption seemed to throw her off. She frowned. "She was to get half, but my room and board was included in that. Now where was I?" she said. She turned to me sharply. "You don't seem very interested."

"I couldn't be more interested."

"Then why aren't you taking any of this down?"

I laughed. "Oh, I never take notes. I work on the theory that if I can't remember it, it's not important—but," I added hastily, "I'm remembering all of this."

I made a mental note not to interrupt again. She continued:

"Anyway, walking through the hotel lobby, I kept thinking everybody was watching me. I even worried about the house detective. Going up in the elevator, I almost lost my nerve. But when I got into the room everybody seemed so friendly.

"There were about a dozen boys sitting around, clean-cut fellows from about twenty-five to thirty-five. There wasn't a gray hair in the lot. They'd been drinking and bottles were all over the place. They'd been to a stag dinner for a friend who was getting married the next day.

"When I walked in, everybody stood up and cheered, like they were at a football game. Then somebody announced:

" 'Here comes the bride—where's the lucky' bridegroom?'

"They all laughed at this, and I laughed, too, and then a tall, good-looking boy stepped up. He was the kid the party was for. I was sure he wouldn't have anything to do with me. But he grabbed me and practically dragged me into another room. I hadn't had a chance to discuss price yet.

"We weren't long. I kept thinking about the girl he was going to marry. Anyway, I was better off than she was.

"When we got back into the parlor, I wondered who was going to pay me. One of the older boys told me not to worry. He asked me what I wanted and I told him thirty dollars a man.

" '*Thirty* dollars,' he repeated pleasantly, 'but don't you think we should get a rate? There's twelve of us here.'

" 'All right,' I said, 'twenty.' It would still come to nearly two hundred and fifty, not bad for a couple of hours.

"I should have known something was wrong when he smiled and said that, since it was a special occasion, I should get fifty from each. He was still smiling as he handed me a fifty. It was the first one I had ever seen.

" 'The bridegroom,' he said, 'should have been on the house—don't you think?'

"By this time I was getting a little uneasy, but I didn't know what to do about it.

"After that they came trooping into the other room. They kept asking if I loved them, and got mad if I didn't respond."

She laughed harshly. "So I'd say I loved them—for fifty dollars, why not? Pretty soon I had five hundred—the older man was the only one who had nothing to do with me.

"I was putting on my coat when he asked:

" 'Did you get enough for one night?'

"I thought he was trying to be nice. I opened my purse to show him. He took out the crumpled bills, counted them, and winked at his friends.

"Suddenly, as I stood there waiting for him to hand back the purse, he drew back his arm and slapped me across the face.

"While I lunged for the bag, two of the others slapped me. They threw the money on the floor, and pulled me into the other room. I fought them until everything went black. When I came to, everybody had gone, leaving the empty bottles, their cigarette butts, and me. I was scratched and bleeding. My clothes were in shreds. I could hardly get off the bed.

"I don't know how I ever got home. I didn't have a penny on me. They'd even taken the money the madam had given me for cabs.

"The madam took one look at me and guessed the rest. She got me into bed, gave me some hot broth and a couple of sleeping pills. Before I fell off to sleep, she told me she'd make it up to me. I wouldn't have to pay for any of the names, and she'd only give me the older men hereafter.

Georgia grimaced. "Some of them are no bargains either. But I'll have to tell you about that some other time."

Weeks passed before Georgia was ready to assume her work. Meanwhile, the ███████████████████████ to get by.

"While I was sitting around," she said, "I suddenly got the urge to go upstate, where I had been born, and find out a little more about myself."

She sensed my sudden interest. "I told you I wasn't like the other girls."

Born out of wedlock and placed in a foster home, she had never given up her restless search for the mother she never knew.

"You probably won't understand how I feel about my mother," she said. "I'll never have a feeling of belonging until I find her or know who she was."

She resented the foster mother because she refused to tell her about the woman she thought might be her mother. "As a small child I remember this woman coming to the house, with little presents, whispering to my foster mother and kissing me. It was only later, when I grew older and the visits stopped, that I started thinking it might have been my mother, and now I'm sure of it. My foster mother kept saying my mother was dead, and I knew she was lying.

"I wanted to be on my own. At thirteen I looked five or six years older, and I knew about boys. I ran away several times, worked as a waitress, and finally my foster mother turned me over to an institution. They got me a job as a maid."

Georgia started going to dance halls with girl friends, the girls dancing together until the boys cut in.

"That," she said, "is how I met Joe. He was my first chance to have a home of my own. He was a sergeant in the Army, but he was getting out. His family said they'd disinherit him if he married me. They didn't know anything about my family—that's all they had against me."

For the first time there was bitterness in her voice. "Anyway, we eloped to Maryland, and I lied about my age. I was fifteen."

From Maryland they had driven on to Florida, where they opened a dance studio. "Everything would have been fine," she said, "but I kept thinking about my mother. Joe couldn't understand, so I never discussed it with him. He was moody, too, and just before he was killed he was complaining that I didn't love him any more. I just found it hard to get excited. When we were first married I acted the way I figured brides were supposed to act, but I got tired of putting on an act after a while."

The casual reference to her husband's death had surprised me. I asked if she minded talking about it.

"Oh, no," she said; "it was long ago."

By this time she was smoking one cigarette after another.

"I was with him when it happened. We were driving down the ocean road for a late snack when he skidded on a wet pavement and crashed into a car.

"They told me Joe died instantly. My arms and legs were broken, and they kept me in the hospital for six months. When I came out I had a limp and didn't feel like dancing."

I asked what she had done about her studio. "Oh, I gave that up. It was getting to be a bore, anyway."

"It was too bad that you and Joe didn't have children."

She suddenly looked as if she wanted to cry. I felt her reserve melt away.

"I was carrying a child at the time. They tried to save it, but it was either me or the child. I guess I was lucky it didn't live, but"—she hesitated—"I would have liked my mother to have seen it."

Georgia had scouted about, looking for means to support herself, when one of Joe's friends arrived from New York and telephoned her. "He asked me to have a drink with him," she recalled. "He was a middle-aged salesman, who had taken dancing lessons from us.

"He had never paid much attention to me. It was Joe he always talked to. We were sitting around having a drink, when he said I ought to come to New York and make some easy money.

"I ignored it. Later, after a few drinks, I wound up in his room because I didn't want to be alone. I thought I might feel guilty on account of Joe. But I didn't feel a thing. It was kind of nice to have somebody around for a change. When he left he gave me his card and said I should call him in New York. I said I'd think about it, and three or four weeks later, when the insurance money was giving out, I phoned from Florida. He told me to come up right away.

"He was at the airport and took me to his apartment. He wanted me to meet a girl friend of his, but she was out of town for a few days. I stayed at his place for a week, and he never came near me. I wondered about it but it didn't bother me. Later I learned that he interviewed lots of girls and got a kickback from the madam. She turned out to be the girl friend. I liked her right away, and moved to her place."

The madam showed more understanding of Georgia's feeling for her mother than Joe ever had. "When I told her I wanted to find out about my mother, she gave me the train fare and a few extra dollars and told me not to worry about it.

"I knew I'd have to trick the truth out of my foster ███████████████████ where my mother had lived. Now, if my mother was dead, as she kept saying, what would have been the harm? I had the idea that she was married and had children, and that's about when the visits stopped, though letters came for years.

"Anyway, when I got upstate, instead of going out to my foster mother's farm, I got the idea of making believe I was my mother. I thought that, before she caught on, she might give something away.

" 'Hello, Ethel,' I said. 'This is Frances. Have you heard from Georgia lately?'

"My disguised voice and the bad connection fooled her.

" 'No,' she said, 'not recently, but I did get a letter from Florida several months ago.'

" 'Well, if you should hear again, let me know.'

"Then my foster mother asked, 'How are the children?'"

"I could hear my heart pounding as I said: 'Fine, they're all fine.'"

"I was praying that she would give me something to go on, but suddenly her manner changed. She broke off the conversation and said she would write."

"The next day I dropped in on her unexpectedly."

" 'Oh, it's you,' she said, 'what do you want?'"

"I think she suspected by now it might have been me on the phone."

"I said, 'I want to know where I can get in touch with my mother. I have to see her.'"

"She looked at me impatiently. 'I've told you a hundred times that your mother is dead.'"

" 'That's not true,' I said, and then I told her about the phone call."

"She said she didn't know what I was talking about. She said she hadn't even got a call. I could see now that she didn't care what I thought, she was determined to keep me from my mother."

"I felt terribly frustrated. 'She's not dead,' I said, 'and you've got to tell me where she is.'"

"She looked at me coldly. I don't think she'd ever liked me, and now I could see the dislike in her face. 'She's dead, as far as you're concerned,' she said. 'Go back to New York and forget her. You've caused enough trouble as it is.' "

Georgia's face hardened and she fell silent. It was now after seven. Georgia looked across the table and laughed. "Once I get started," she said, "I can't stop. That's the story of my life."

She checked her watch. "Have to run," she said. "I'm late as it is."

I wanted to ask a few more questions. She nodded toward the bartender. "Well, he can tell you where to find me."

As she stood to slip into her coat, I said, "Just one thing, what ever happened to your father?"

She seemed surprised. "Nobody worries about their fathers, do they?"

It was two weeks before I saw Georgia again. I discovered that she lived in a small midtown hotel on the West Side. "Be careful when you call her there," the bartender said, "they'd throw her out if they knew about her."

I managed to reach her after three or four attempts. "I can't talk now," she said, "but meet me at five tomorrow at the hotel bar."

I arrived promptly at five, but Georgia wasn't there. Inquiry at the desk revealed that she had not been in all day. The room clerk couldn't have been nicer—too nice. "Maybe she's on the road," he smiled, fluttering his eyelids.

I was noncommittal.

"These actresses," he said, flinging up his arms effeminately, "always on call, always having to be someplace, always busy, busy, busy."

I wanted to laugh in his face.

Not really expecting any results, I nevertheless left word for Georgia to call me at my office.

Three days later, she called. "I had to go out of town," she explained, "something I couldn't pass up. I'll meet you anywhere this afternoon."

I suggested the bar where we had met the first time; she had seemed at ease there.

She was only five minutes late; she looked strangely different. Then I realized why. There was a small bruise under her left eye, her jaw was swollen, and the skin over her cheekbones was lacerated. She explained.

"I went down to Philadelphia for the weekend with these two characters. The money was good, but I'm not sure it was worth it. They were a couple of degenerates."

"How did you happen to make the trip?" I asked.

"Oh," she said, "I was sitting in a bar one night with these two jokers, and they got to talking about doing something different. They came from Philadelphia and wanted to show me the town."

She grimaced. "What a town!

"We stopped at the first motel on the way, took separate rooms, and then all piled into my room. They were real gone. For a while I thought they liked each other more than they liked me. Then this one guy kept wanting me to hit him with a belt. When I wouldn't, they belted me instead."

She sighed. "It's things like this that make me think of settling down with one guy."

I asked if she had any prospects.

"Well, there's this one fellow I like. He usually takes me to the track for luck. He's a bookie, and has money. He gives me a hundred or two to bet with, and if he has a really good day he gives me more. The only trouble is, if he finds out what I am he'll drop me fast. Not that he'd care himself, but he wouldn't like some of these other Broadway characters to have that on him."

I mentioned that a well-known jockey had been happily married for years to a former prostitute."

"I'm not worrying about marriage," she said. "It's just that I get sick and tired of knocking around bars, drinking when I don't feel like it, and trying to be clubby when I'd rather be in bed alone."

"Didn't the bookie ever want to know what you do for a living?"

"I told him I was still collecting on my husband's insurance," she laughed, "and then as a cover-up I took a job for a while in a five-and-dime. But it was too much, getting up when I didn't get in until late."

"But how do you avoid him?" I persisted.

"I only hit the East Side bars," she explained, "just a few small places where I'm well known. He's a West Side kid. The danger isn't running into him, it's running into the Johns when I'm with him. But as long as I see them first I'm all right."

I recalled that she had said something earlier about a party for older men. She smiled. "I'm glad you reminded me, I get a kick just thinking about it.

"Before I broke up with Cathie—the madam—she asked me if I would go to another party.

" 'No more parties,' I said and meant it.

"But she laughed and said this was different, just a bunch of old fogies who had a night out and wanted a chance to show they still had something left. She said she'd be surprised if there was anybody there under fifty or sixty.

"I asked how much was in it, and she said I could probably do pretty well, particularly if I acted like a lady and didn't say anything about money."

The affair, Georgia told me, was held in a leading hotel under the sponsorship of a group of executives in the garment industry, honoring the man who had done the most, in their opinion, to bring glory to the industry.

Georgia smiled. "I wasn't invited to the dinner. There was an after-dinner celebration in one of the upstairs suites, and that's where I was the guest of honor.

"There were five or six men in the suite when I came in. They stood up and I gave them a quick once-over. They were all pretty old and tired, but they seemed to come to life when I walked in. I could see them all running their eyes over me, peeling my clothes off, and yet not being too obvious about it.

"They were all fat and bald, except for a couple that had fringes of gray hair, but as men go, they weren't bad. They were the kind that thought of themselves as solid family men, and I guess they were. Anyway, the man who had been the guest of honor was now playing host. He put on a nice little act. He bowed over my hand, and then turned to his friends. 'Now this is a guest of honor we can all appreciate.'

"They all laughed, and then I could tell they had been drinking. About three or four of them tried to get a chair for me and couldn't have been nicer.

"Nobody seemed to be in a hurry. They kept asking me questions, but I was used to that by this time. Anyway I gave them a brief history of my life, making it a real tearjerker.

"They actually seemed interested. When I got through, one of them—a nice old man with glasses that were always falling down his nose—threw his arms around me and said, 'You poor girl.'

"If he could only have seen how silly he looked.

"Two of the other men decided they didn't want me to go into the other room with them. They said something about how society had done enough to me. They were pretty silly, too. But I felt better about it when they said they'd pay me anyway.

"Things were getting pretty maudlin when another of the men finally laughed and said:

"'Gentlemen, I make a move that the two guests of honor get together for their own good.' This went over pretty well, and everybody laughed.

"Anyway, we went into the other room. The others made out they didn't see us leave. I got the feeling they were all a little embarrassed and, if they hadn't been drinking, might have just left the money and run. I don't know whether they were afraid of their friends knowing, or were just afraid of knowing themselves, or were afraid of me.

"When I started taking off my clothes, I could see this man getting flushed and uncomfortable. He started talking about his daughter, and how she was just about my age, and how we even looked alike. I thought he was trying to get out of it. But then I discovered he was only embarrassed about telling me what he wanted to do. I wasn't shocked."

Georgia shrugged. "How long can you keep getting

shocked? Anyway, it was obvious there wasn't much else he could do.

"We were in the room for a half hour. Then two more came in, and it was the same all over again. I hadn't said anything about money and neither did they. But I got fifty from each of them, and the three others who didn't do anything gave me fifty each, too.

"Then they started to leave. None of them looked very happy. I could see them going back to their fat little wives and feeling like they were unclean all over.

"The man whose suite it was got me in a corner and told me he wanted me to come back in an hour, after everybody had left. He had made a big point of not going in with me.

"I kissed everybody goodbye, and dropped around to a bar nearby for a drink. When I came back, he talked to me for two hours about his wife and kid and about his business. It was a dreadful bore and I wondered when he was going to get to it. He told me he didn't have anybody to talk to. His wife was busy with bridge and golf and art. She sounded like the typical wife of the typical John.

"This would have gone on all night, but I was getting tired. I said I'd like to get to sleep. That brought him back to reality.

"When I did get to bed, finally, I had a hard time getting to sleep. I didn't like the idea of lying there all night, but I hadn't got my money yet and I didn't want to do anything to curb his generosity. While he was lying there snoring, his mouth open, and his false teeth on the night table, I got up and went into the living room. I listened to the radio, read magazines, and got myself exhausted so I could crawl back and doze off.

"In the morning, when I woke up, he was gone. But there, on the pillow next to me, were two hundred-dollar bills. There was a little note, too, printed—I guess he didn't want his writing on it. It said: 'For being such a nice girl.' "

I thought for a while. "It sort of made up for the other party," I said, "didn't it?"

She looked up with an enigmatic smile.

"I don't know," she said, "they were both pretty much the same."

CHAPTER 10

Shortly before the second Jelke trial, a well-known man about town telephoned to ask if I would be interested in some inside information on the case.

I felt that the story had been pretty well covered. "No," I said, "but I might be interested in talking to some of the Jelke girls."

"What for?"

"Well, they're an articulate lot, and they might have some idea of why they're doing what they're doing."

He laughed derisively. "Don't you know?"

I was about to hang up when he said quickly:

"I know just the girl. She writes poetry, goes to the opera, reads all the time, the intellectual type."

He laughed. "You two can discuss Spinoza together."

"Keep Spinoza out of this," I said. "He never did anything to you."

I suggested a luncheon date. "Hell," he said, "she doesn't wake up until dinnertime."

We arranged to meet the following evening in a cellar restaurant on the West Side, a few blocks from the girl's apartment.

They were both there, in a corner booth, when I arrived. Jack took charge of the introductions. The girl was easy to look at. She was a vivacious redhead, and in the dim light seemed hardly out of her teens. She wore no make-up except lipstick, which exaggerated the line of her full lips. Her hair fell loosely over one shoulder. She acknowledged the introduction with animation and said she enjoyed meeting writers.

Jack, a hulking fellow with little tact, interrupted gruffly:

"Yeah, but all this one wants is to write something." He laughed at his own joke.

It became apparent that Jack would dominate the interview. Whenever I asked a question, she looked at him inquiringly.

As we ate, I studied her closely. The lines around her eyes and mouth told me that she was older than I had thought.

She smiled impishly.

"How old do you think I am?"

Jack looked up crossly. "Who was talking to you?"

She sat back, subdued, but I said, "Oh, about twenty-four."

My reply pleased her. "I'm thirty-one," she said, looking defensively at Jack. "Now guess how old my son is."

Jack slammed his spoon on the table. "Look," he said, "he doesn't want to know your life story, all he wants to know is why—"

There were not many people in the restaurant, but Jack's voice was beginning to attract attention. "Let's just finish dinner," I said, "and I can talk to Peggy some other time—alone."

"That's all right with me," Jack said. "I just don't like her being so damn fresh."

When I visited Peggy at her apartment three nights later, she took me into the living room, apologizing for the general untidiness, and offered me a chair that must have been designed for midgets.

She laughed and clapped her hands. "I'm only five-two," she explained, "and Jimmy is about the same."

"Jimmy?"

"Oh, that's my son. He's fourteen. He's liable to be coming in any minute."

I hesitated. "Does he know about you?"

She shrugged. "I don't know. I usually go out, but I guess kids hear things they shouldn't."

She mixed a highball for herself. "There's enough for us both," she said, "but don't tell Jack. He didn't want me to drink while you were here."

I declined, and she downed both drinks.

Peggy looked as if she'd had a rough night. There were circles under her eyes, and her hands trembled when she reached for a cigarette. She looked tiny in a dark frock that hung on her slight figure. She pointed with a smile to a nonexistent bust line. "I've lost so much weight that nothing fits any more."

Although she had had formal education, she spoke meticulously, occasionally spicing her conversation with slang.

"My great trouble," she said, "was loneliness. I'd do anything not to be alone, even live with a man who bored the hell out of me."

A sound at the door caused her to look up. "That must be Jimmy."

A short, husky boy entered the room and greeted me without surprise. "Jimmy," his mother said, "did you bring that bike back?"

"Yes, mom," he said. "It's back."

He was a good-looking boy with red cheeks, blond hair, and a firm chin. After bustling about for a few minutes, he announced that he was going to the movies with George. "A friend of his," Peggy explained.

"All right," she said, "but come right home after the show, not like the other night."

When the door had slammed, she turned to me wearily. "I don't know what I'm going to do about him. He's almost too much for me." She sighed. "And he's getting old enough to understand."

She laughed. "He and Jack argue all the time like a couple of kids."

I wondered how Jack fitted into the household, but felt that it would eventually come out.

"Would you like to see my poetry?" she asked. She brought out a large cardboard box, crammed with papers, and handed me two or three pages. The writing was barely legible, and the rhyme was bad.

She watched me closely as I read. It was pretty stark stuff, with a strain of suicide running through it. "You seem fascinated by the East River," I observed.

She laughed. "They say people who talk about suicide never do it."

"Anyway," I said, "not while they're talking."

There were fragments that dealt with frustrated love, with girls she had liked, with men, but none of it went anywhere.

When I had finished, she carefully put her poetry away. "Jack said I should tell you anything you want to know, but there's a lot of things I wouldn't want him to know. I used to live a lot fancier than this. But I take what I can get now. You can only drink so much booze, be with so many men, and go to so many parties—one day you've had it. I used to know the best, Hollywood, New York, Chicago, London, Paris—I went everywhere and did everything. I could have married again, but they were too old or too dull, or not right for Jimmy."

"You must have been a kid when you married," I said.

"I was sixteen, and I didn't know a thing about sex. I found out I didn't know a thing about marriage either. Frank—my husband—raped me on my wedding night, and he kept raping me night after night. He was fourteen years older than me. I thought I was grown up marrying an older man. But I hated him from the time he ripped off my clothes and forced me. 'Go ahead and rape me,' I thought, 'see what good it'll do you.'

"I didn't want his child, but didn't know how to avoid it. The next time I got pregnant I fell down fifteen steps and then crawled up and fell down again, just to make sure."

Color had come to her face. Her eyes glistened and she looked alive. "Is that the kind of stuff you want?" she asked.

I nodded, asking the familiar question, "How did you happen to get into the business?"

"Well," she said, "after I left Frank I landed a job as a hat-check girl in a night club. I liked being around clubs, there were all kinds of characters there. But the pay was only thirty a week and it cost me that to board Jimmy."

After work, Peggy had dated the black marketeers, cloak-and-suiters, and playboys who patronized the club, their pockets fairly bursting with cash.

"I didn't take money at first," she recalled, "not outright. But we'd get to talking about my son and they'd say, 'Here's ten for cabfare,' or maybe it would be twenty. At parties, sometimes, I'd be the only amateur. One night a blonde got me aside and said, 'If I looked like you, I'd be sleeping in mink.'

"That," she said, "is how it started. I began taking fifty, and then a hundred, and for a while I could almost name it. I had twenty chances to go out for every one I took."

There was something about her story that puzzled me. "I don't understand how you could simply leave your husband and become a prostitute. Emotionally, I mean."

She shrugged. "That's how it happens to most of the girls."

"But you said your husband was the only man you knew?"

"You're trying hard to be the reporter, aren't you?"

"Not particularly. It just puzzles me."

"All right," she said, "can I trust you?"

"You're not even using your real name," I pointed out. She began to giggle. "All right, you're the first one I ever told this to. There were other men when I was married. And do you know who the first was?—the iceman. Isn't that a howl? I just hated Frank so I had to get even. But aside from that, I got no satisfaction out of it. The iceman was a nice boy though, and a friend of ours. Later he sent his brother over with the ice." She laughed. "I guess you might call it a family affair."

Subsequently, Peggy got a divorce and gained custody of the child.

"He said he never wanted to see the child, if it meant seeing me. I don't know what he was so mad about. If it wasn't for Jimmy, I could feel as though we were never married."

Few men had made an impression on her, and those who did, she conceded, were the ones who treated her badly.

"I had no use for anyone else. I lived with a man for twelve months and wouldn't let him touch me. He'd get my breakfast in bed, massage me, help me dress. He'd get so excited he'd shake all over. I had to laugh when he told me he loved me. But I finally got tired of the silly business and checked out. A psychiatrist once told me I subconsciously saw my father in this man, and was trying to get back for my childhood when my father wouldn't even look at me."

She paused. "It sounded like rot to me. What do you think?"

"I don't know," I said. "I'm neutral."

She brought out another bottle of whisky and poured another drink for herself.

"What else?" she said, making a face as the whisky burned her throat.

"I was thinking about Jimmy."

She bristled. "I was a good mother," she said. "Most of the money I made went on him. I never thought it would be permanent. I figured I'd save enough to quit or else get married. As a matter of fact, I did quit twice. I was making better than a thousand a week at the time, and gave it up, but it didn't do any good.

"I took Jimmy with me wherever I went. I kept him in foster homes on Long Island, and this meant pulling him in and out of school. He must have been in twenty homes before he was seven, but if one weekend went by without my seeing him, he'd carry on terribly.

"I wanted to send him to a good school, a military school, where he'd grow into a real man. I didn't want him on the streets. But the money slipped through my fingers. Somebody was always in trouble—my married sisters, my mother, even my friend the iceman and his family. Nobody liked the way I made my money, but they didn't mind taking it."

"And you did it all for Jimmy?"

"Oh, no, I liked the gay parties, the happy times, the sense of irresponsibility, the successful people, the feeling of doing anything when I was drinking, but it was mostly Jimmy."

It was a problem, she acknowledged, protecting Jimmy from being involved in her frantic existence, particularly at the time she was sharing living quarters with a petty gambler named Ralph.

"Ralph," she explained, "came with me when Jimmy was about seven or eight. I told him that Ralph was a friend. I didn't want to lie and say he was an uncle or anything like that, and besides I didn't like living alone. It made me moody. I had thought of sharing with another girl. But how could I bring up a boy with two prostitutes?"

Every evening before she left she would slip into Jimmy's room, kiss him as he slept, and murmur, "Always remember that your mommy loves you."

She met Ralph at a party. "He was the most beautiful man I'd ever seen, almost like a woman. He had never worked in his life. There were a dozen girls dying to support him. I never found out what he liked about me.

But I got more kick out of his knocking me around than from other people being nice to me."

Ralph was useful in many ways. "I met a lot of people through him, big people. He knew them all. He knew the madams, too. One day one of the madams who used free-lancers called me. She knew Ralph. She had a big deal for me—a Jersey millionaire who wanted somebody for two weeks, two thousand a week. It had to be the right girl. The madam told me this guy was a pushover for the girlish type."

Peggy's eyes met mine. "That was a few years ago. I couldn't have looked more than eighteen."

"You don't look much more now."

She seemed pleased. "Anyway, I had to go over to Newark, which was really the end, but I couldn't turn down that money. I checked into the John's hotel, and waited for the phone to ring. The madam said he had to be careful because he was married and a civic leader." She laughed. "That always gets me about these civic leaders, all their concern for their reputations."

She poured another drink. "He wasn't bad-looking," she said, "about fifty, tall, gray at the temples, the distinguished type. But when he saw me he was thrown for a loss.

"'Why,' he said, 'you're practically a child!'

"He kept asking me questions, and I gave him the kind of story I thought he'd like—real hearts and flowers. Then, after a couple of drinks, he kissed me on the forehead, and sent me back to my room. My first surprise. The next day we went over to New York, shopping. He really splurged, a fur coat, dresses, shoes, underthings, even a ring.

"That night he told me about his wife. It was the same old beat-up story. They were married in name only, but he couldn't get a divorce because of the children. Only the windup was different. He wanted to buy a home for me and the boy—I had told him about Jimmy.

" 'The only thing you won't have,' he said, 'is marriage.' "

Peggy looked at me, trying to judge my reaction. "Do you find that hard to believe?"

"Why should you make it up?"

"I haven't. That's just the way it happened—and do you know what?" Her eyes brightened. "I could have married him, and I'd be Mrs. Rich Bitch today."

She resumed her story. "I said I'd think it over. Meanwhile, nothing was happening. It was the strangest thing. I was beginning to think I was losing my appeal. But one night, after some drinks, we were sitting close on the davenport. I started fiddling with his vest. For all his talk, he was no different than the others. One of my girl friends used to say, 'There's two kinds of men, the live and the dead.'

"When I got back to my room, I started thinking about Jimmy and Ralph. I put through a call. When I got Ralph on the phone, he started kidding me about the John. He asked me if I was falling in love. We both laughed. He told me to hurry back with the loot. I kissed him over the phone and hung up.

"I hardly put down the receiver when the John walked into my room. I thought he was going to cry. 'Why did you have to do that?' he said.

" 'I'm sorry,' I said. 'I didn't know you were tuned in.'

"When he kept looking at me with those sheep eyes of his, I got mad. 'I can't help it,' I said. 'It's part of being a whore.' He winced as though he'd been slapped.

"I slipped the ring off. He didn't even hold out his hand. He was still standing there when I walked out the door."

Meanwhile, Jimmy was showing his first resentment.

"One afternoon," Peggy said, "I overheard them arguing and Jimmy called Ralph a pimp. It made my stomach kick over. The next morning Jimmy had a big welt on his face. I guess Ralph had walloped him when I got out of the house.

"That decided me. When Ralph was out, I packed our things and Jimmy and I headed for the Catskills. I had been thinking about it for some time. I took a job as a waitress at a resort hotel—twenty a week, tips, and board for us both.

"Tips were good, for a waitress, but I almost broke up one day when some guy—a real John—plunked down five dollars on the table and expected me to jump for joy." She laughed. "I've gotten five-hundred-dollar tips for less."

But the job ended in the fall.

"I boarded Jimmy out again. I was afraid he was getting too old to be with me all the time. But we spent Christmas together, in Florida. I had been invited down, but I couldn't go without Jimmy. We had always been together for the holidays."

The John, an elderly industrialist, had welcomed Jimmy.

"I have nothing against kids," he assured Peggy. "I have a couple myself."

Peggy smiled at the recollection. "I'd spend all day on the beach with Jimmy and meet Sidney after he put his wife to bed. He couldn't stand his wife's whining. 'What I like about you,' he'd say, 'you never complain. If it's cold, it's her arthritis; if it's warm, she can't breathe.' But Sidney paid me well not to complain. The only trouble was, he was always reforming me.

" 'You ought to get married,' he said, 'before your boy knows what you're doing. You'll never convince him you did it for him.'

"Back in New York, I got to thinking. I decided I'd better get Jimmy into school somewhere. He was almost twelve and could hardly read or write."

"Wasn't it embarrassing," I said, "to have a son that big?"

"Most of the Johns didn't know." She sighed. "But you're right. How can you stay twenty-two, with a son twelve?"

"Does getting older make any difference?"

She laughed. "Doesn't it make a difference with you? Sure, I got tired, tired of bouncing around every night, tired of trying to be pleasant, tired of passing from one date to another. There were days when I felt too damn sick to get out of bed. For the first time, it occurred to me that it might be nice to have somebody take care of Jimmy and me. If I could have had that guy from Newark, I think I'd have grabbed him right then. Instead I ran into a crooner, and was with him three months. But he wasn't a real John. He'd give me an occasional fifty or a hundred and laugh, 'This is between friends.' If he had been a girl, I know what he would have been. We had an argument one day and he disappeared for three weeks. When the hotel manager said he had given up his suite, I got the message. I needed something fast, and by luck"—she smiled, "you know, I am lucky—I ran into a girl friend who said there was somebody special she wanted me to meet. He was a racketeer, but he owned night clubs, restaurants, and apartments, like all those racketeers.

"He was the first big-timer I'd ever met. We had dinner at one of his restaurants. He didn't look like much. He was dark and husky and he didn't do any talking. But it was his eyes. They didn't look at you, they looked through you.

"I knew I had registered. I always knew. Before we got through dinner, I was telling him about Jimmy and wanting to send him to a military school."

" 'All right,' he said, 'how much?'

" 'Five hundred,' I told him, 'for the first term.'

"He handed me five new bills. They were so new they stuck together."

Suddenly, Peggy came to a halt. "You haven't said anything. Are you sure this is what you want?"

"Tell me about Jimmy," I said.

She seemed pleased. "Well, it's nearly all Jimmy. It's a funny thing about Jimmy and Dick; they hit it off fine at first. I was afraid Dick was going to spoil him. When we visited Jimmy at school, Dick was loaded down with presents. But when Jimmy came home for the summer, the trouble started. He was jealous of Dick. He tried to ignore him and I could see Dick doing a slow burn. I got Jimmy aside and told him he should be grateful.

"He'd look at the floor, and say, 'Mommy, why can't we live by ourselves? I can sell papers or run errands or do anything.'

"I asked Dick if he would marry me, but he was satisfied the way things were. Shortly after that, Dick and Jimmy argued about watching a television show, and Jimmy didn't come home later. I called the police and they found him sleeping in a hallway. He kept running away. I wanted to go back to work, but Dick wouldn't let me. 'Not while you're with me,' he said.

"So Jimmy and I ran away, to a small rooming house across the river in Queens. I found a job as a receptionist, but I couldn't stay well enough to keep it. While I was sick, Jimmy was an angel. He waited on me night and day, made the meals, did everything, but it couldn't last.

"People like Dick don't let anybody leave them, they leave you. He pulled a gun on my girl friend and found out where we were. When he walked in, Jimmy got between us, but I made him leave the room.

"Dick said if I wanted, he'd get a divorce and marry me. That was the first I knew he was married. Funny thing, I had never thought of him as a sweetheart. For a tough guy, he didn't know much about love. Sometimes I embarrassed him."

Abruptly, she stopped talking, and sank her face into her hands. All the animation oozed out of her, and when she lifted her head she looked tired.

"The day we went back with Dick, Jimmy disappeared.

Two weeks later the police in Pennsylvania picked up two boys in a stolen car. One of them was Jimmy. That was too much for Dick, so he took off. I had to take Jimmy to court. Later, the probation officer got me aside and said that Jimmy needed a strong hand, a father or somebody else who could handle him."

"And what happened?"

"Nothing yet. They wanted me to call Jimmy's father to see if he would take him. Otherwise, they said, an institution might be best for a while. Until he gets over the difficult age."

She turned to me. "What do you think I should do?"

"Nobody can make that decision for you."

There were tears in her eyes. "Jack says a reform school would do him good, but he's not bad, really."

Awkwardly, I wished her luck. She had regained her spirits and squeezed my hand at the door, saying she hoped we would meet again. "I got a sister that I know you would like."

I thought this was the last of Peggy, but the next day Jack called.

"Did she tell you anything?" he asked.

"Yes," I said, "she was articulate, but not a Jelke girl."

"The same thing," he said. "And what did you think of the little monster?"

"Who's that?"

"Jimmy, who else?"

"He seemed like a nice boy."

"Nice boy, just stole a bicycle last week, a real juvenile delinquent."

A week or so later the pieces fell into place. The phone rang, and it was Peggy. The name meant nothing until she said she had something to add to her story, and could we meet for a drink, anywhere?

She greeted me warmly and ordered a double Martini. She looked chic but still tired. Mentally, I compared her with the other women in the room and found her no different, except that she was prettier.

"I thought you would want to know the rest, since you were interested in Jimmy," she said.

I waited. She was obviously disturbed.

"This afternoon," she said, "I brought him to his father's and said goodbye. He said he would take Jimmy if I kept out of his life. I had to promise, what else could I do?

"He hadn't changed much, just a little older and meaner looking. He pushed Jimmy into the house and slammed the door in my face."

She began to cry. "I had to promise I wouldn't even write him. I know Jimmy will understand. It's for his own good." She dabbed at her eyes with a crumpled handkerchief and abruptly changed the subject.

"Have you heard from Jack?" she asked.

"He called."

"Please don't tell him you've seen me. I've moved and don't want him to have my address."

"You better not tell me, then."

She wrote it out. "You might have a few more questions. I've been trying to lose Jack," she explained. "He's a nice guy but I can't afford him. I left word with the answering service that I was in California. The other day I get a message to call somebody I had never heard of before. I thought it might be a new client. But when I said hello a voice said, 'So how is California?' It was Jack. I'm getting the phone changed. I'd just like some peace for a while."

As I settled the bill, she smiled, putting her hand on mine. "Jess, I wonder if you could help me? You know how upset I've been over Jimmy. I haven't been able to do anything and don't have the first week's rent."

She was still smiling, her hand on mine, patently wondering how much the traffic would bear.

Finally, she said:

"Oh, twenty would be fine."

I handed her the money.

"I certainly enjoyed talking to you, Jess," she said. "You can interview me anytime."

CHAPTER 11

It was still not apparent to me why some girls became prostitutes and others never could, given similar circumstances, environment, and temptation.

Almost every girl I had spoken to thought she had the answer. I was not so sure.

I watched Eileen closely as she recalled her career. She was only nineteen, a call girl for less than a year. She was still new enough, I thought, to remember every terrible detail of her decline.

She came from a good family. Her father had died when she was very young and her older brothers had

▆▆▆▆▆▆▆▆▆▆▆▆▆▆▆▆▆▆▆▆▆▆▆▆▆▆▆▆▆▆▆▆▆

"I'd rather not talk about Mother," she said. "Anything else, and you can have it."

She was blonde, with blue eyes, a soft voice. She was not pretty but was *simpatico*, a quality usually associated with the Latins.

She was sitting opposite me in her apartment. The place looked as though she hadn't got around to furnishing it yet.

"If you want to know how a girl becomes a prostitute," she said, "you came to the right person. I don't see how anybody could know if I don't."

I had been warned that she was highly excitable and had to be handled with care.

I decided I would let her ramble on, steering the conversation only when it came to a standstill.

She told me that she had arrived in New York nine months before, leaving home after she had been raped by a married man with whom she had thought she was in love.

"I was silly enough to think he loved me. He was married but separated and said he was getting a divorce for me. We were out this one night in his car, and he kept begging me. When I said I wanted to wait, he got mad, beat me up, and later threw me out of the car. I wound up in the hospital. But you would have thought I had done something to *him*, the way people looked at me, particularly my brothers. I had never had an experience with a man before, and they were treating me like I was a whore."

The memory seemed to overwhelm her. She brushed her hand over her eyes. "It made me feel unclean. I still feel unclean. I don't think anything can ever make me clean."

Her voice was rising.

"I try not to think of it, just as I try not to think of how many men there have been. I counted them until I got to fourteen, and then I stopped. I just can't accept it."

Abruptly she began talking again about the man she hated. "He was going on trial for what he had done to me, but everybody was against me. They tried to get me to withdraw the charge, saying that I shouldn't have been going out with a married man. My brothers said I was disgracing the family. I had so much pressure on me I didn't know what to do.

"Only my mother stood with me. She told me to do what I had to do. For two weeks before the case was to come up, I couldn't sleep. Then one night I took some sleeping pills. The doctor got there too soon."

She was unable to appear in court, and the case was adjourned. Rather than relive this ordeal publicly, Eileen finally decided to leave home. Her brothers were relieved —only her mother cried.

Eileen was now speaking with great intensity. Occasionally she jumped to her feet and paced up and down the room, and then flung herself back into the chair. It was a strain just watching her.

"I had about two hundred dollars when I arrived in New York," she said. "I didn't know anybody here. I just wanted to get swallowed up in the city, forget everything I had gone through and everybody.

"I asked the cab driver if he knew a good cheap hotel. He knew just the place. He hung around while I checked in, but I finally got rid of him.

"The next day I went looking for a job at the employment agencies. I guess they were bad agencies. The men there kept telling me I was wasting my time. They kept asking me to lift my skirt, so they could see my legs. A couple of them suggested that I start as a cigarette girl or camera girl in night clubs.

"I finally got a job as a filing clerk in a Broadway office. I always kept hearing the same thing: 'You're wasting your time, with your looks and figure.'

"I didn't pay too much attention. Meanwhile, I'd met a fellow in the hotel. He had been standing around in the lobby when I checked in, and later when I was paying my bill at the cashier's window, he was right behind me.

"We got to talking and he took me out a couple of times. He told me I was wasting my time, that with my looks I didn't have to work for thirty-five a week. He took me to a bar near Times Square, where I met an older woman, a redhead.

"She wasn't like the men. She didn't beat around the bush. She said that if I went to work with her—not *for* her, mind you—she'd see that I made a good thing of it.

I'd get half and she'd get half—but it would be a big half all around.

"At first I didn't know what she was talking about. I thought maybe she meant hustling drinks or something like that. Then it dawned on me.

"When I said no, she laughed. 'You're a dumb kid. This city is full of suckers, and there's no harm in taking a sucker. In a few years you can tell them all to go to hell.'

"This fellow kept telling me I was a fool, too. 'Why worry about money,' he'd say, 'when you can have all you want?'"

Eileen seemed calmer now. She went to the refrigerator and came back with a bottle of beer. "That's all I'm drinking now," she said. She split the bottle between us.

"Did you ever see that woman again?" I inquired.

"Not to talk to, but I've seen her around, and I've thought of her because of something she said."

I looked up.

"Oh, it was nothing." Eileen shrugged. "Just when I was leaving her that night, she sort of smiled at me and said, 'You're going to eventually, you might as well start now.'"

It was soon after this that Eileen fell in love. "I started going out with this boy I met in the hotel bar. He was sympathetic and I trusted him. I got to thinking that maybe men weren't so bad. But then I told him about the thousand dollars I was supposed to inherit when I was eighteen. He got me to ask for it. He said he'd invest the money for me, and that was the last I saw of him or the money.

"I don't know whether I was weak or stupid or what, but everything men did made them seem more hateful. I finally started thinking that maybe that redheaded woman was right. The hell with them. Why shouldn't I make them pay for what they'd done to me?"

"Were you still working?" I asked.

She nodded. "But I wasn't making enough to live on. I

was flat broke. This first fellow I had met at the hotel—the one that introduced me to the redhead—said he would line up the men for me—all good people: businessmen, buyers, socialites. By this time I figured it didn't matter much what I did. You can only give yourself away once, anyway.

"I bought this list of names from the fellow at the hotel, ten dollars a name. I didn't want to go into the red too much, so I only took fifteen names. I was to pay him back out of what I made.

"He told me to charge from twenty-five to a hundred dollars, or whatever I could get—mostly though I got fifty to sixty."

I was surprised at the quick transition from office girl to call girl.

"Didn't I tell you that everybody kept after me all the time?" Her voice cracked. "They got me so confused I didn't know what I was doing. If they'd only let me alone."

I apologized for not following her properly.

"Where was I?" she asked.

"You were just starting your career."

"Oh, yes," she said. "I'd call these men, the ones on the list, say I had just got into town, use a certain girl's name —it was like a password—and say she had suggested I call.

"The Johns were all happy to hear I was in town. There was one man, though—quite famous—who said he'd rather visit me than have me visit him. I told him I wouldn't have anybody at my apartment."

She smiled for the first time. "You're the only man that's ever been here."

It struck me as a dubious distinction. "Do you remember your first experience?" I asked.

"Do I remember it? How can I forget it? I knew so little about sex that I became pregnant from my first date."

This seemed almost incredible. "Who was the man?"

"Oh, he was an older man, about fifty. He lived on Park Avenue and had lots of money. He could have been worse, and, as I look back, I can see that he made it easy for me. I didn't let him know he was my first, because I thought he might pay me less."

"But when you told him you were pregnant?"

The question appeared to upset her.

"I never told him about it. It was none of his problem. In fact, I never saw or heard from him again. I guess he thought I was too inexperienced. Two months later I had an operation."

Meanwhile she had broken with the procurer who had put her in business. When she mentioned his name her blue eyes clouded with anger. "One day I went up to his room to pay him off. He was there with a friend of his. They started messing around and, when I resisted, they tried to force me."

She clenched her teeth. "I guess they knew they'd been in a fight—the pigs. They couldn't be satisfied with just their money."

I was puzzled. "But why did it make so much difference to you?"

She started to cry. "It's bad enough to be a prostitute, without everybody rubbing your nose in it. They were making fun of me, and I wouldn't let them.

"I don't think of myself as a prostitute," she sobbed. "I never use that word in thinking of myself. Maybe I'll get used to it, but now I think of myself as a girl who got lost and may still find her way."

"Why can't you get out? You're still a kid."

She shook her head mournfully. "My priest has tried to help me. I don't know what I'd do without him. I talk to him all the time. He wants me to go out West and get a fresh start. He told me I could stay with relatives of his out there.

"But I don't want to be under obligation to anybody. And what could I do—work in a department store?"

"It seems a good opportunity," I ventured.

"You don't understand," she said. "I'm not ready for it. I feel too dirty to live a conventional life now. I've made my bed and I'm going to lie in it."

"But you're young enough to marry and have children."

"Look, I don't want to get married and I don't want any children. I don't want any kind of lasting relationship with any man."

"You've liked men before," I persisted. "They can't all be bad."

She thought for a while. "I suppose that about ten per cent of them act like human beings. Some of them, particularly the older ones, aren't so bad. But I don't know, they're still taking up the same time.

"The other night a real old guy took me to a night club, bought me dinner, gave me fifty dollars, and put me in a cab.

" 'If I had a daughter,' he said, 'she might be just like you.' "

Eileen's eyes brimmed with tears. "Funny thing, I cried all night thinking about it.

"But that isn't what usually happens. The other night I was at a bar, and a drunken old slob came over to me, started pawing me, and said:

" 'I'll give you anything you want.'

"I had his number right away. When he wasn't drunk, he was the kind that wouldn't give away the right time.

" 'Let's not talk about it here,' I told him, 'I'll meet you outside.' "

She laughed. "I gave him a little chuck under the chin to keep him happy. Then I walked out and he followed. He was staggering so he could hardly make it. I told him that it would cost him fifty dollars, but I'd have to have part of the money now. I gave him a phony room number, a phony name, and a phony kiss, and he gave me thirty dollars."

I was surprised at her candor. "I've done it a number of times," she said, "and I'll continue to do it. It always gives me a feeling of satisfaction."

Other girls, less attractive, earn more.

"I don't make as much money as some of my girl friends," she told me, "because some days I just like to be alone or go shopping.

"I don't know what I average. I've never figured it up. I don't work Sundays. I go to church in the morning and run through the Sunday papers in the afternoon. That's the day I save for myself."

CHAPTER 12

When the Jelke case broke, a new household term was coined around the country—it was "Jelke girl." Not everyone was sure what it meant. It was loosely used to describe not only the glamorous call girls who served Jelke, but any high-priced prostitute who traveled in café society.

The Jelke case itself came as a shattering blow to the so-called Jelke girls. The devastating spotlight found many of these ████████ facing themselves for the first time. It was more than they could stand.

A few turned to religion, recoiling from seeing themselves as the world saw them. Others fitfully tried acting, dancing, singing, modeling. Some tried losing themselves in prosaic occupations. The more desperate turned to marriage.

Generally, however, there was no sincere wish for reform, and the Jelke girls bitterly resented everyone who had anything to do with their exposure. They railed against the prosecutors who forced them to testify against Jelke—and against Jelke himself.

Many jeered at the picture drawn by the State of Jelke as a big-time procurer preying on young girls.

"Mickey Jelke," said the girl sitting across from me, "was a jerk trying to play big-shot.

"There is no question that he took money from some of the girls—I saw him do it myself—but to say that he made any of these girls prostitutes is ridiculous. They were call girls, most of them, because they were too lazy or shiftless to be anything else. And if there hadn't been a Jelke, they'd still have been call girls, only they wouldn't have done as well."

I was not particularly interested in the Jelke case. I had written about it and felt that if the Jelke name had not been so well known it never would have made headlines.

However, the stunning impact of the publicity on the girls did engage my interest and was my reason for pursuing the subject.

Nevertheless, I was mildly surprised that the fresh-complexioned blonde, nonchalantly chewing a wad of gum, should be so critical of her sisters.

"I have only contempt," Dorothy said, "for girls who can't handle their business. Nobody with half a brain would require anybody like Mickey Jelke."

She was lolling in a chair, dressed in a smart suit open at the throat, crossing and uncrossing her legs. Although she was at least thirty, she had ████████ outdoor look—from golf and tennis, I later learned—and the good muscle tone of the professional dancer.

She was not impressed by reporters. She said drily: "Some newspapermen wanted to ghost a book I'm thinking of doing, but I'd rather have a first-rate writer—or do it alone."

I couldn't suppress a smile, and this seemed to annoy her. "Everybody," she said, "knows that newspapermen are limited, or they wouldn't be newspapermen. They'd be Steinbecks or Hemingways."

"They were both newspapermen," I said.

Frank, the man who had helped set up the interview, was fidgeting in his chair. He turned to the girl, irritated.

"If you don't want to answer his questions, say so."

"All right," she said, "what's the question?"

I didn't see any need for mincing words. "What did you need Jelke for?"

The answer bounced back. "I didn't. I made the mistake of helping one of his girls. I took her in when she didn't have a place to stay and she started bringing men to the apartment. That's how I got involved.

"She was a ██████████████████████████████, and she threw it in his face. It fell to the floor and laid there, until I picked it up. It was ridiculous. She didn't have the brains to make fifty dollars a month at anything else.

"She didn't stay long, two weeks, but it was enough to tie me up with her. I couldn't stand her around. She was dirty. She never washed, and she left her things all over the place."

She laughed bitterly. "And yet when the case was on she was the big glamour girl, posing for all the pictures, while the rest of us were trying to pull our coats over our heads."

Suddenly she looked. "I thought you weren't interested in the Jelke case."

"I'm interested in what happened to the girls."

"Like what?"

"Well, like what happened after your pictures got in all the papers, and everybody knew who you were. I understand you had stood pretty well socially, belonging to country clubs and all that."

"Yes," she said, "that all went out the window. I had always lived a sort of double life, like a lot of girls. The people in one circle accepted me as they found me, a pleasant, attractive girl who could swim, play tennis, and talk."

She shrugged. "When the case broke, I didn't even bother to find out if I was still a member. I knew that life was all over.

"I was a curiosity wherever I went. Everybody seemed to recognize me. When I strolled down a street, walked into a restaurant, or stopped for a package of chewing gum, I could feel everybody staring at me. Sometimes men came over and said hello."

She paused a moment. "Hell, they wouldn't have had enough money to know me."

"I was beginning to feel like Hester Prynne, with a scarlet letter on my forehead.

"My landlord had made me move—after first propositioning me, of course. I went to a small hotel, where I thought nobody would know me, and began hunting a job.

"After three weeks, and still no job, the manager called me in and said I'd have to leave. Somebody had told him who I was. He said it didn't matter what name I used or how I behaved, he couldn't afford to have me there."

She laughed mirthlessly. "I felt like asking him how he meant that. He gave me three hours to get out.

"Frankly, I was a little desperate. I didn't have much money, and a man I thought I could count on turned against me when I wouldn't marry him."

She explained:

"Before the trial I had to pawn some jewelry. I left the tickets with him, because he went my bail. He got so mad because I wouldn't marry him—the slob—that he redeemed the tickets, married somebody else, and gave her the jewelry. A real John.

"I didn't feel like working just then, and thought I'd better get out of town. I headed for Miami. It was the same there. I took a small apartment, and after two weeks the landlord recognized me from a story in some cheap magazine. He asked me to leave—after the usual proposition, of course.

"I made carfare and went out to the Coast. I was pretty well known around Los Angeles, and thought my friends might help me. I dyed my hair and changed my name. I had so many names by this time, I couldn't remember which I was using where.

"Through friends I got a few bits on television, and

was getting around to where I could almost support myself.

"But the news got around and the casting director got word from his boss—no more TV for me.

"Then I got a few traffic tickets, and the police recognized me and asked me to get out of town."

She laughed gratingly. "I almost forgot about my interlude in Chicago. Do you want it?"

I nodded.

"Having friends all over, I called up this guy in Chicago and he said to come out—he'd find something for me. He was part owner of a coal company and he gave me a job selling coal over the telephone. You would think that nobody could have possibly objected to that. But a couple of the other partners found out about me, and I got fired.

"Later, the firm went out of business, but they couldn't blame me. I sold coal like mad."

Frank, our mutual acquaintance, had wandered out of the room. When he came back, he said, "How about Las Vegas? Did you tell him about Las Vegas?" He turned to me. "This girl has really had a rough time."

"Don't anybody feel sorry for me," she said. "I'll manage."

"What about Las Vegas?" I asked.

"An old friend connected with a Las Vegas hotel arranged for me to get a job as a chorus girl in his show. I had been a dancer when I first started out, and I thought I might be able to get back in the swing.

"It took about two days for the usual trouble to start. Funny thing, the men were all right, it was the other girls who raised hell. You would have thought they were angels, the way they looked at me, instead of what they really were.

"They made things difficult. They gummed up routines I was in, told the stage managers I was too old, and, of course, wouldn't talk to me. The managers didn't want to come right out and fire me, because of my friend and because they didn't like anyone to think they weren't running the show.

"But they began giving me the toughest routines in rehearsal, work that kids ten years younger would have had trouble with. At the end of the day I was so weary I just collapsed, but I wasn't going to give them the satisfaction of quitting. Nobody was making it easy for me, why should I make it easy for them?

"This went on for days. Finally the director put it on the line. 'Look,' he said, 'there's too much pressure on me. I can't keep you in the show. Sorry.'"

At this point, desperate, she began thinking of going home. "I hadn't seen my mother in fifteen years," she recalled. "She was a marvelous woman. For years I sent money back. She thought I was doing great, dancing, in TV and the theater. I don't think she thought of it too much. My father could never keep a job. I didn't worry about what he thought.

"But it must have been a shock to see their daughter staring up one day from the morning paper. Mom got on the phone and told me there was always room for me at home."

Dorothy suddenly got up. "How about a drink?"

Frank fixed a Scotch on the rocks.

"That was the worst of it," she said, "Mother knowing about it."

She turned to Frank. "What else does he want to know?"

"Why don't you ask him?" he replied, nettled.

"All right," she said, "so I'm asking him."

I had sensed her hostility. I thought it might be because I was a newspaperman, and therefore identified with her exposure. It was illogical, since I had not covered the case itself.

However, it reminded me of the time when I was a very young reporter covering a prostitution case in police court.

An old madam, just convicted, was being led down a hall by a bailiff. She noticed me and stopped.

"Say, sonny," she said, "have you been writing all those stories about me in the papers?"

"Well, yes," I said. "I've been calling them in."

"So you're the son-of-a-bitch that's been causing all my trouble." And with that she hauled off and walloped me across the face.

The bailiff dragged her away, screaming imprecations.

When I looked around, my face red from more than the slap, I could see the judge laughing. He had witnessed it all.

"What are you laughing about?" I said. "You sent her away."

"Hell," he said, "she'll be cursing me for the next thirty days. Everybody's to blame but them."

All this passed fleetingly through my mind as I studied Dorothy. But aside from a hardness, which she made no effort to conceal, Dorothy could have been a society girl having her cocktail before dinner.

"Well," she repeated, "any more questions?"

"Yes," I said, "one thing puzzles me."

She looked mildly interested.

"I can't understand why you were broke after all these years."

"That's easy," she said. "I don't think anybody did any better, but I spent it when I had it, and there were a few bad investments."

"What kind of investments?"

She seemed annoyed. "Does it matter?"

"Oh, why don't you tell him?" Frank cut in. "What difference does it make?"

"Well," she said, "I put a couple of friends in business, and they weren't as smart as they thought they were—they lost everything."

"Men or women friends?"

"Men, of course. As a matter of fact, they were boy friends."

"What did you want a boy friend for?"

She looked at me scornfully. "What do you mean by a question like that?"

"Well, most of the girls seem to have nothing but contempt for men."

"That's for Johns," she said impatiently. "That has nothing to do with being in love."

"Don't tell me that you were in love."

She turned to Frank. "Who is this joker? He doesn't know anything.

"Of course, I was in love, lots of girls are. What do you think I gave this boy all my money for? I certainly didn't do it for laughs."

I shrugged. "That's what I'm trying to find out."

Her voice was harsh. "Then listen awhile and you may learn something. You'll never learn anything talking.

"Twice I set this boy up in business. It took practically all my savings." She looked up. "That would be more than a newspaperman would ever get to see in his life."

"That wouldn't be difficult," I said.

"Anyway, when it failed, I didn't give him hell like another woman would. I took a place near Palm Springs, and we stayed there until he got over the disappointment."

"Didn't he have any money of his own?"

"No. He gambled a little, but he had never worked, aside from the two flyers he took." She pursed her lips. "Maybe that's why he failed—he didn't have enough experience. But he had a good head on him."

"If he never worked," I persisted, "you must have supported him."

She really got angry. Her face flushed and she gulped down her drink. "You're like the rest of the reporters. If a story doesn't suit you, you make it up."

"It's the only inference I can draw."

"Why draw any inferences?" she shot back.

"Okay," Frank cut in, "so you didn't support him—he just lost your money for you."

He turned to me. "You see, Dorothy figures that if the ventures had worked out she'd have more than got her money back."

She appeared somewhat mollified.

"I only have a few more questions," I said. "Do you mind?"

She shook her head.

"Where is this fellow now?"

"In Florida. I might join him later."

"Well, if you were in love with this man, why didn't you marry him?"

"For two reasons," she said. "One, he never asked me, and, two, I'm not sure I loved him enough. But maybe I'll change my mind if things don't improve."

"You've never been married?"

"No. I just never met anybody I cared that much for. If I do, I'll get married." She looked up at me. "You don't have to worry about it."

"Only two more questions," I said.

"I know," she said. "How did I happen to become a call girl?"

"That's the first."

She crossed her legs. "It's the usual story. I thought about it again in Las Vegas, when those idiots in the line were giving me a hard time.

"I started in a chorus, too. After the shows, just like the other girls, I'd go out with the rich boys who had been sitting around waiting for the break.

"I discovered that if you were nice to them, there might be a diamond ring, or a necklace, or a mink coat. We never got paid much, just enough for the rent and for coffee and sandwiches."

She laughed. "When you got the job, that's one of the things they told you—the pay wasn't much but you could name the tips.

"Pretty soon some guy was helping me with the rent, somebody was giving me money to send home, somebody was paying for my clothes. It seemed silly to say no, when they were springing for champagne like mad and me with maybe seventy-five cents in my bag."

"How long did this go on?" I asked.

"Oh, maybe a year. Then one day I was getting ready for a date. I was wondering what kind of an evening it would be, and suddenly I saw myself in the mirror.

" 'By God,' I thought, 'I'm a whore.'

"I gave up the chorus job. I was always careful and few people knew I was in the racket until"—she grimaced —"that damn Jelke case."

She looked up inquiringly.

"My last question," I promised. "I remember your saying that you sometimes got girls for old customers of yours—technically, wouldn't that make you a madam?"

"No," she said crisply, "not technically, or untechnically either. I told you that I tried to help other girls, and it didn't do any harm to please my Johns. They always liked a change, and they'd eventually come back to me. There's more than enough Johns to go round, believe me.

"And," she added coldly, "I didn't *get* the girls, as *you* say, I only suggested that they call. I didn't get anything out of it."

That was the end of the interview. The next day Frank called and said, "Dorothy thought you were too damn fresh."

"Well, I didn't exactly think she was the Queen Mother. And, besides, she wasn't leveling."

"What do you mean?"

"That bit about bringing in other girls just because she liked them."

"It could be," he said. "She comes up to my place because we're Bohemians—nobody thinks anything of her being a call girl."

Subsequently, I was talking to a newspaperman who

had known Dorothy. He had just come in from the West.

"I wonder what ever happened to her," I said. "She was talking about getting married the last I heard."

"You're kidding," he replied. "Hell, she's got herself one of the best stables of girls in the country."

CHAPTER 13

Although I doubted that a Jelke girl differed greatly from her sisters, I thought there might be variations in personality and attitude that would throw new light on the problem. I also wondered if any of the girls publicized in the Jelke case had reverted to prostitution or whether the shock of public exposure had been enough to cause their retirement.

I had learned that one of the girls was writing a book on prostitution to support herself and her small child.

"It's a curious thing," my source said, "she's about the fifth Jelke girl I've heard of that's writing a book."

"I should think they would be happy to be forgotten."

"Well," he said, "now that they're celebrities they figure they might as well make the most of it—and they've got an idea they can get by until the heat is off."

When I called his friend Betty, she said she would prefer to see me at my office. "It might be a trick, and I'm not walking into any traps."

She was not quite what I had expected. She was about twenty-six years old, dark-haired, with a round face and ▮▮▮▮▮▮▮▮▮▮▮ She was pleasingly plump and reminded me somehow of all the stories I had heard about farmers' daughters.

She shook my hand firmly, looked about curiously, and asked whether many people in the office knew I was interviewing prostitutes.

"Just about everybody," I said.

"Isn't there a private office we can go to?"

We adjourned to an executive chamber.

Before I could ask a question, she said: "I think I might as well tell you I'm not like the other girls. I've been studying my problem, particularly since the Jelke case shook me out of my trance, and I can tell you why the girls behave the way they do."

She seemed supremely sure of herself. "I know you've talked to a lot of girls, but they don't know any more about it than I did before I snapped out of it. They're all sick, just like I was sick before I went to a psychiatrist, and he made me understand what I was doing. Now I'm well again, writing a book, and thinking of getting married."

"What's the book about?"

"Oh, about me, the other Jelke girls, and how they're all sick—sick, sick, sick." She laughed suddenly. "It's wonderful to see it clearly for the first time and be able to laugh about it."

"I'd like to see your book," I said.

"Not a chance. Everybody wants to see it. If I show it to you, what'll I have for my publisher? But maybe you can see parts of it, if you promise not to use any."

"What was your connection with Jelke?"

After a few seconds she answered.

"I knew Mickey Jelke but I never worked for him directly. I was a Jelke girl in the sense that I exchanged phone numbers and went on dates with the other Jelke girls. There was a whole circle of them. However, I stayed out of the smart supper clubs. I didn't like parading myself the way some of them did. It was bad enough, without advertising it."

Recalling that she had a child, I asked, "You were married once?"

"Sure," she replied, "that's how I got into the thing in the first place, and that's how I got my child. I wouldn't want anyone saying my child is illegitimate."

She smiled knowingly. "I know what you're driving at. You want to know why I'm thinking of marrying again.

Well, just ask me. You don't have to beat around the bush with me. I'll answer any question if I want to."

"All right, why are you getting married?"

"This time it's a little different. I'm not in love or anything like that, but this man is very nice, he likes my boy, knows all about me, and wants to make me happy. It isn't easy when you've got a child and have never learned a profession. I went to college for two years, but I didn't get much out of it."

"How have you supported yourself?"

She hesitated. "Oh, hell, I might as well be honest. When the stories broke, I moved out of my apartment into a low-cost development with my kid. I got myself a job as a secretary. By the time I got through paying the baby-sitter, I had only a few dollars left. There were days when there wasn't even milk in the house. I applied for relief, but nothing happened. If we had waited for them we'd have starved to death."

Her voice rose sharply. "I wish you'd get that in about the relief department—they really tried to humiliate me."

She brooded for a moment.

"If it hadn't been for them, I might not have gone back to seeing a few men. I had to be very careful because I was afraid of the police, but we had to eat. I couldn't let my child starve."

"Is that how you met the man you're thinking of marrying?"

"No," she said; "he was a friend of somebody I was seeing. But, I told you, he doesn't care about that. Before my awakening I couldn't have made any man happy, because I short-changed them all. When I made love, it was as though it was all onstage and I was a spectator. Now I find myself remembering what a failure I must have been as a call girl."

"Failure?"

"I don't see what emotional or intellectual satisfaction anybody could have got out of me," she explained. "I made no effort to know them as people. It was purely a physical thing, and the quicker the better."

She looked across the desk, blue eyes twinkling. "I told you I'd made a study of this—now do you believe me?"

"Not particularly."

She drew back as though I had slapped her.

"What do you mean?"

"Since we're being so frank—"

"Now you're being sadistic," she said. "I thought reporters were impersonal."

"All I want to know it what happened to you. You're too close to it to analyze it yourself."

"You don't know what you're talking about. They say a girl gets callous in the business. That isn't true. You get more sensitive. You are always watching to see whether people look down on you. You seem to get more hard-boiled but that's only a cover up, a sort of defense mechanism."

"Well," I said, "let me ask you a stock question."

"Go ahead," she challenged.

"Why couldn't you go out and work like other women for your child and yourself?"

She was so angry that she could hardly talk.

"Let me tell you about these other women," she said finally. "I met them when I moved into that tenement building. Most of them were like me, separated from their husbands, living there with their children and not doing very well. Somehow they found out who I was, even though I had changed my name.

"When three or four were together, and I walked by, their noses hit the sky. But the same women came to me one by one and asked me how they could get into the racket. They were sick of doing without things.

"What a joke! They were all so plain that the Johns I knew wouldn't have bothered with them for free. And, obviously, they didn't know what they would be letting themselves in for. All the while *I* was a call girl *I* was looking for an out.

"I was too strong to take dope or drink—or maybe just scared—so I went to a psychiatrist. I had to, or I'd have gone out of my mind. I got a lot out of it, as you can see, but I got to thinking it was ridiculous to continue to have relationships with men so that I could pay the psychiatrist to tell me why I was miserable having relationships with men."

She got up and walked to the window. "I think that I'm one of the few girls who knows enough of her case to understand why she became a prostitute. It's like everything else, it goes back to your childhood.

"When I was fifteen I was so melancholy and depressed I felt like committing suicide. My mother got to worrying about me. She took me to one of these Park Avenue quacks and he told her that what I needed was an affair."

She laughed bitterly. "But I can't blame my mother. She wasn't very stable.

"One night she brought this boy up to my room and left us. But then she must have got frightened, because she came back in a few minutes and took him away."

She sat down again. "If I'd had a real father, it would never have happened. My stepfather was a monster. Behind her back, he was always trying to accommodate the psychiatrist. I managed to fight him off, but it was wearing—physically and mentally.

"I was ready to commit suicide. But, as long as I was going to kill myself, I figured I might as well give sex a try first. Everybody seemed to regard it as a cure-all."

At this point she fell silent. I thought she might want to continue at some other time.

"Oh, no," she said, "I was only thinking how one thing leads to another and before you know it you're hooked."

She resumed without emotion:

"I lost my virginity at sixteen. It was a great disappointment. In fact, it started new complications. It brought on my guilt complex. The man was young, but still several years older than I. After that there were two or three more, and the guilt complex kept growing every time I stayed with a man.

"I finally married the first one, because my family didn't approve and because somehow I thought I would right things inside by marrying the man who had given me the guilt complex."

She laughed. "It makes me shudder when I think of what a fool I was in those days. But this man filled a need in me for somebody of my own, and if he'd been different, it might have been all right.

"You see," she explained quietly, "he's the one that made me a prostitute—on our honeymoon."

"On your *what?*"

"You heard me," she said harshly, "that's my one claim to fame."

"How did you happen to agree to anything like that?" I asked.

"Well, he didn't just come out with it. He planted the idea, gradually. We had been in Florida a week, at an expensive hotel, and I was wondering where the money was coming from. One night we saw a girl pick up a guy at the hotel bar. That was the incident my husband was waiting for.

"The next night he seemed preoccupied and I asked if something was wrong. The more anxious I got the more reticent he got, until I finally squeezed it out of him. He said we had run out of money and he'd probably go to jail for bad checks.

"Naturally, I said I'd do anything to help. He kept saying no and I kept pleading. Finally, he said there was a way I could help, but he didn't like to ask. So, of course, I made him ask me. When he saw my face he said he was sorry, but he had thought it would be easy, like the girl at the bar the night before."

"And you fell for that?"

Her impatience was thinly concealed as she replied, "I told you I must have been sick, but I sold myself on the idea that by being a martyr I would keep us together. I cried all night and he held my head.

"The next evening I went to a hotel bar, and that started it. It never got easier. I never went out with a John that I didn't break down in tears at a critical point. A lot of Johns liked this. They thought it was passion—and that made them more generous."

I still didn't understand how it was possible for her to live with and bear the child of a husband who had made her a prostitute.

"How can you be sure that the child was your husband's?"

"Oh, everybody's asked me that. It's really quite simple. I didn't give the Johns anything of myself, and made sure they didn't give me anything.

"It wasn't until after the Jelke shocker that I came to see Johns as people—always before I had thought of people as Johns. I had never bothered trying to know any of these men. But I have since, and, believe me, many of them are more pathetic than I ever was. I really don't hate them any more. I pity them.

"You know, in my book I'm having a couple of chapters on Johns. That'll be a twist, since they usually write about us."

"Why bother? They sound pretty obvious to me."

She stared at me with contempt. "You're a fine person to be doing this story. You ought to have a girl helping you."

"I've had many." I laughed.

She replied scornfully, "You don't know enough about psychiatry, psychology, and things like that—you're not the type."

I explained that it was not a reporter's job to interpret. "I'm not trying to be an authority. I am merely trying to learn why a girl becomes a prostitute."

"Well," she said, "it's evident you don't know much about Johns, if you think they're obvious. Most of them are just as sick as the girls. They're either schizophrenic, psychotic, or just plain emotionally disturbed—and this reliance on call girls is one of their symptoms. They could go out with other girls, but they get more satisfaction out of us. That's because they're masochistic, or sadistic, or both." She radiated smugness. "I told you I was hep on the subject.

"Let me tell you about this one John. He came from a social family, one of the best, but I got to feeling sorry for him, despite his millions and his Newport connections. Nobody loved him for himself—and on top of it all he was horrible looking and thought everybody was after his money.

"He might have been better off if he'd had something to do. Every morning he would go down to his office, sign a few papers his lawyers put in front of him, then take a big spyglass and watch the waterfront for hours." She giggled. "You should have seen his eyes light up when he talked about the boats." She seemed to find something amusing.

"He was a strange one. After watching the ships, he would go home and supervise the preparation of his lunch. This was a big thing with him, since he couldn't stand meat or eggs. He was such a nut about eggs that he didn't even like people who ate eggs."

She laughed. "He wouldn't vote for Eisenhower, because Eisenhower came out for eggs.

"Every afternoon after lunch, he'd put in a call for a girl. It might be me, or maybe two of us, but not at the same time. Having a call girl over was as important as ordering the right thing for lunch. Then he'd have dinner out somewhere, generally with the second girl, and get home by eleven. It was important to him to get home by that hour. He prided himself on his schedule.

"He was always snapping at his chauffeur or his valet,

but he was always willing to listen to a girl's problems. You could tell he was genuinely interested."

"With all his money," I said, "I suppose he was quite generous."

She laughed. "Not him. He was generous with gifts and things like that, but he was strictly a fifty-dollar John. He never paid more, though he could have paid anything. It was against his principles. And, for that matter, with his fortune and prestige, he could have had any girl he wanted. But call girls filled a need in him. I guess they made him feel wanted.

"You may not believe this, but he wanted me to marry him—before all the Jelke publicity, of course."

"Well," I observed mildly, "it might have been an improvement."

"My husband wasn't the problem. I was separated by this time, but I wanted to think it over. He wanted to take me to Europe for the honeymoon. I told him I'd let him know when he got back. Well, while he was on his way over, the case broke, and that ended that.

"I heard from him, but he never said anything about marriage." She laughed again. "It would have been a bigger story than the Jelke case."

The sequence of events puzzled me. "I had understood you were still with your husband."

"I was," she said. "We were separated, but I was working with him. I had to do something to support my child. Later, when my eyes were open, I got a divorce. I understood for the first time that I'd been sick. Maybe I'm still sick, but only a little."

After a slight pause she added brightly:

"I've even got to thinking lately that I'm well enough to make somebody a good wife."

"How about the man that wants to marry you?"

She hesitated. "Well, I'd like to see first how I do with this book. And there's another problem. I didn't mention it before. There's really two men, and both know my past.

"I asked this one guy whether he could overlook or forgive what I had done. He said there was nothing to forgive." She quoted him as explaining: "Since what you have done and what you have been through have made you what you are."

She frowned. "I'm sure he means it now, but I'd like to know him better. I've got a few things to work out for myself, too. I've never known a prostitute who didn't hate herself for what she was doing. I've never known one who doesn't remember the first time with a pang. And I've never known one with a past—because it's never past. There isn't a girl that doesn't want to get out. I'm trying, and with God's help I will."

She stood up, adjusted her picture hat, and drew on her gloves.

"I never want my child to think of me as a prostitute."

A week later I called her again to ask if she would pose for a picture to illustrate her story. "It would be from the back, and nobody would know who you were."

"Then why don't you just use anybody?"

"Because it would be more effective with you."

"Can't you say it's me? Nobody would know the difference."

"That would be misrepresenting, and no good newspaper would do that."

"All right," she agreed finally. "I'll come down, for a modeling fee."

She named a figure, to which I agreed, and I had the impression, immediately, that she regretted not having asked for more.

She looked cool when she arrived, although the day was quite warm. She was well made up and appeared much younger than her twenty-six years. As the photographer got ready, she turned to me and asked, "How can I be sure that my face won't show?"

"We'll be very careful."

"Somebody might still recognize me."

"Well, you might hold your face in your hands, as a precaution."

She held out her hand to stop the photographer. "With all this risk I should have more money."

I explained that I could pay only the agreed amount. The photographer observed helpfully:

"Nobody can recognize anybody in newspaper pictures anyway—how could they know you from the back?"

I counted out the money that had been promised her.

"Why not have the picture taken, and then we'll make up a few prints and use only what you approve?"

"All right." She accepted the money.

When the pictures had been developed, she selected two with great care. We put them aside, discarded the others, and I escorted her to the elevator. It had been a trying two hours.

But I had not heard the last of Betty. Shortly after the articles appeared she telephoned.

"Do you remember that book I was writing?" she asked. "Well, we've decided against having it published."

"Who is we?"

"The man I've decided to marry. We're going to get married next month. You know, the one I told you about."

She laughed. "I decided I wasn't any sicker than a lot of wives."

I waited.

"Anyway," she went on, "he got to worrying about the book, and we went down to the publisher's together. But the publisher wouldn't agree to the changes."

"That's too bad, after all you put in it."

"Yes," she agreed, "but I think I can salvage some of it." She paused. "I thought maybe you could use parts of it after the changes were made."

"I don't see how, at this time."

"Your articles weren't bad," she conceded, "but I

think my material is much better. Not because of the writing," she added quickly, "but it does come from somebody who's been in it." She laughed. "Sort of from the horse's mouth."

A month later I called her to ask if I might see her manuscript.

"I'm sorry," she said, "but my husband made me burn it. We were married last week."

The receiver clicked gently in my ear.

CHAPTER 14

The case histories in this book have been selected because each girl is typical of her trade and yet dramatizes some special facet of the general problem. Her thinking may be faulty and distorted, but she is not mentally retarded and usually knows where she is going. Yet, frequently, I found myself wondering about what a girl had told me. While many girls talked frankly, they were often self-deluded and overly concerned with impressing their audience. This was part of their problem. For example, when a girl told me she hated men it was apparent to me as a reporter that she was only telling me what set her off to advantage.

While there was a definite behavior pattern in them all—B-girl, pony-girl, streetwalker, or call girl—I could only speculate about the motivation. I was a reporter, not a psychiatrist, and quite frankly I did not understand the psychological difference between girls who became prostitutes and others with similar backgrounds who did not. The dividing line seemed fuzzy and uncertain. But of one thing I was sure, without fully realizing its significance at the time: not one of all the girls I had met had come from a happy home.

The behavior pattern did not vary from girl to girl— an underlying hatred of men, a lack of zest for sex, an unmistakable undercurrent of lesbianism, a strange attraction for unfortunates, a distorted devotion to pimps, addiction to drugs or alcohol, a marked suicidal strain, professed disinterest in marriage and motherhood, and thinly veiled contempt for women not like themselves and for society in general. And, above all, there was a consuming loneliness, marked by constant flights from reality. It was commonplace to find prostitutes on sleeping pills. As a matter of fact, I was referred to a psychoanalyst regarded as an authority on prostitution by a call girl who told me:

"Don't write anything without talking to this headshrinker. Anybody who can take a pros off sleeping pills is a wonder."

"Don't expect too much," the analyst warned when I called on him. "Not enough prostitutes have sought analysis to allow us to generalize with assurance."

"How about all the women who have been arrested and questioned by city psychiatrists?" I asked.

"It all depends on the psychiatrist's ability to evoke the girl's candor and cooperation when she is already smarting with resentment at her arrest and on how much confidence the psychiatrist can develop in her."

However, I had found that psychiatric results can be startling.

"Hell, my headshrinker helped me too much," Mazie told me. "After six months on the couch—and paying for it, too—I discovered I was beginning to like my work. It gave me the shakes. One night, this kid looked at me and I flipped—first time since the high school prom. Later, I could hardly get dressed, I was so nervous. I didn't even wait for the money."

Mazie never went back to her analyst. "I wasn't going to let that happen again," she said grimly.

The analyst nodded. "That would be typical. These girls do not go into analysis because they want to stop being prostitutes. They come here because they've reached a point where they can't eat, sleep, or work, and are finally forced into analysis as a last resort. Their sense of guilt is so great at this point that they're on the verge of suicide."

The analyst, too, had found prostitutes essentially alike.

"The prostitute is consistent in that she's everything but what she seems to be. Instead of loving men, she hates them. Instead of being oversexed, she's undersexed. Instead of being frivolous, she's burdened with despair. The sex act means no more to the average prostitute than the act of washing her face. She sells neither her body nor her soul—only her time."

"But why bother with men at all?" I asked.

"It's a matter of revenge, though most prostitutes don't realize this themselves and profess a purely commercial interest in males. Actually they get their only satisfaction out of hurting and deceiving men. They are sick women bent on self-destruction, and they first destroy what men prize above everything else in a woman—female virtue."

The girl's hatred of men, he felt, was part of a compelling need to debase the father figure. Many of the girls I had interviewed spoke fondly of their mothers but mentioned their fathers only with contempt or scorn.

"Without exception," the analyst said, "these girls have a weak father symbol. Most of it goes back to childhood when they first began to resent their fathers."

I asked him about a girl who had remarked bitterly that her father had always ignored her.

"In early childhood, this rejection by her father was unconsciously a sexual rejection and would tend to repress her normal sex desires as she grew older. In all her subsequent relationships, she is striking out at the father figure. While repressing her sexual feelings, she views her clients with contempt, and the more animal-like they are the more satisfaction she derives from her own detachment."

"And the father?"

"Each time she degrades a John it is her father she is subconsciously degrading."

I told him about Peggy. She had despised her father because he drunkenly forced himself on her mother. Her mother, finally, was unfaithful to him.

"This made him doubly contemptible in Peggy's eyes —because of the mistreatment and because he was too blind to see what his wife was doing behind his back."

Peggy had described her husband by saying that he was as bad as her father, and that he made her feel like a prostitute.

"As she grew up and married," the analyst said, "this contempt for her father apparently blossomed into resentment of males generally. However, as a virgin she was not aware of her own repressed hostility. The husband obviously couldn't reach her, nobody could have, and it made him a savage. The girl wasn't aware that it was essentially her fault, but she couldn't have helped it even if she had known. All she knew was that sex left her cold."

The analyst pointed out that both Peggy and her mother had followed similar patterns of revenge. External circumstances (the need to support herself and her child), however, had triggered Peggy into a career of prostitution.

"But for all we know, the mother was saved from prostitution only because she was too old to set out for herself. Neither Peggy nor her mother derived any sexual satisfaction from their extramarital relationships. They were too clearly motivated by revenge."

This explanation recalled Peggy's grim admission of her first revenge. "That first man I cheated with never realized what he had done for me." And she would have taunted her husband with her infidelity had she dared. "But it wasn't worth being killed for."

On the analyst's couch, prostitutes make no secret of their contempt for men. A former patient, a $50 girl, had told the analyst: "When they keep asking if you love them, I want to throw up, but I run my hands through their hair if they have any and tell them they're cute—the monsters."

"How do you account for the fact," I asked, "that these

girls feel so superior to the man when they seem to be doing what he wants them to do?"

"That," the analyst explained, "is one of the keys to the riddle.

"Whatever the price, the prostitute never thinks of herself as submitting to the male. When she appears to be yielding most, she is actually most triumphant, since she has stirred her adversary without being stirred herself. Businessmen, actors, politicians, doctors, lawyers, schoolboys—it doesn't matter who they are. All are fair game, including reporters and psychoanalysts. No one" —he grinned—"is exempt."

"I got that impression, too," I agreed, "and it puzzled me, since I was in a position to expose them."

"So was the missionary in *Sadie Thompson*—and look what happened to him. You were a challenge—the detached observer sent out to interview the lowly prostitute. What better game could she have?"

"It doesn't seem like much of a victory," I said dubiously.

"I can assure you," he said, "that it is nothing else. Actually I have never met a prostitute who would admit she had enjoyed an act or intercourse."

Because she gets no satisfaction out of men, the prostitute usually turns to women, generally prostitutes like herself, who represent the comforting mother image.

"With other prostitutes," the analyst said, "she may find companionship and some sex satisfaction. Nearly all prostitutes are lesbians, or soon become lesbians, and get a curious pleasure out of having men support these secret relationships."

Since she gives men so little of herself, it is entirely possible, the analyst said, for a prostitute to carry on simultaneously with her regular Johns, have girl friends, keep a pimp or shower her affections on some unfortunate.

I had witnessed some of this generosity myself. I had seen girls stop in the street to drop coins in the cups held out by blind beggars. I had seen others stand entranced as cripples sang carols or played violins for handouts. I had seen a B-girl rush up to a legless mendicant on a roller-skate platform and plant a kiss on his bared head.

"In view of their hostility to the male, how do you explain this kindness," I asked, "unless it's all a grandstand gesture?"

"Although she preys cheerfully on the predatory male, the prostitute is paradoxically generous with unfortunates. The disabled, the impoverished, the underprivileged can all expect special consideration from her. It is terribly important to her that she be important to somebody—if it's only a stray cat. It is probably the only situation in which she is capable of tenderness for the male, although she often deludes herself into thinking that she can love like other women."

He mentioned a typical case—a girl for whose time men were eagerly bidding. But she preferred a hunchback who had saved up $100 for their first date. "After I got to know him," Francie told the analyst, "I tried giving back the money, but he wouldn't take it." There were other peculiarities. "He never wanted to go out because he felt people would know I was a prostitute. No other kind of girl, he said, would go out with him."

She looked forward eagerly to their meetings, brought him little gifts, showed him rare tenderness. "He was the only man I ever knew who liked me for myself, not sex. Mostly we sat around and talked, but I stayed over if he wanted me to—something I did for nobody else."

It didn't last. The hunchback, given new confidence by the call girl's interest, soon found a girl who wasn't a prostitute and married her.

"It gave her quite a shock," the analyst said, "but she seems to be pulling out of it."

For weeks she had mumbled, punishing herself, "How could anybody love a whore?"

"The word acts like a lash on these girls," he explained, "whether they use it on themselves or somebody else does.

"Actually, the unfortunate takes the place of a pimp, who, of course, would not tolerate such generosity in one of his girls—toward anyone else, that is."

"That's another relationship I want to discuss," I said, "the prostitute and her pimp."

"The motivation is comparatively simple," he explained, "though the girl herself seldom understands it. One reason for the association of prostitute and pimp is the state of loneliness in which women begin as prostitutes, when they are unsure of the step they have just taken and require constant reassurance.

"But above and beyond this, through her association with the pimp, the prostitute manages to achieve her supreme triumph. Far from being a symbol of affection, the money she gives the pimp represents the utmost degradation she can heap on the male. At last, without deluding herself, she has created a male image to which she is clearly superior."

A call girl, with rare insight, had told the analyst: "You say I am subconsciously seeking to degrade this pimp. I say there's nothing subconscious about it. It gives me satisfaction every time I throw his dirty money at him."

These relationships are rife with violence. The prostitute apparently glories in being mistreated and her "old man"—as the pimp is significantly known—glories in mistreating her. "His beatings meant more to me than other men's kisses," Alice confided. "When he wouldn't beat me, I knew he didn't care."

The fact that she was only one of many girls apparently heightened Alice's interest. It also led, one night, to a bizarre situation. She was with her "old man" in his hotel when there was a sudden rattle at the door. Through the panel a girl whispered that she had some money for him.

"Throw it through the transom," he said. Before day-break three more girls rapped at the door, threw their money in, and stole away. "I was lucky," Alice said, "to get there first."

The pimp serves another purpose, too. He provides the prostitute with the verisimilitude of a normal male-female relationship, thus allowing her to cling to the fiction that she is little different from other women. And when the relationship ends, shattering this fiction, the prostitute reacts with typical violence. Many attempt suicide. "With some of these girls," the analyst said, "the world ends every day."

The slightest upset may lead, characteristically, to a suicide attempt. "I had just got home from a party," one girl told him, "and was feeling good because everybody had been so nice. I got to thinking I wasn't so horrible, after all, when the phone rang. It was a John. He wanted me to get over right away. I said I was tired, and he asked what from. I said I was to this party, and he laughed. I didn't see what was so funny. 'Can you see those chins dropping,' he said, 'if they knew you were a whore.' When he hung up, I felt like turning on the gas."

I had noticed that many suicides had a history of dope or alcohol.

"Drugs and alcohol," the analyst explained, "will help to break a girl down, particularly drugs. However, if neither existed, we'd still have prostitutes and they would be trying something else. Generally, the prostitute turns to drugs or drink to escape from herself, and when these fail she may turn to suicide, since she can never quite convince herself that she is anything but what she is."

As a last sop to her self-respect, however, the prostitute usually refuses to perform at least one act in her burlesque of love. Often she will resist, violently, any man who attacks her standard. "In this way," the analyst observed, "she deludes herself that she is one cut above some other girl."

One of his patients had drawn a knife on a John who offended her. "As soon as I came into the John's room," she said, "he told me to do something I wouldn't do for any man. When I backed off, he called me names and cuffed me across the face. I picked up a knife from the table and told him I'd kill him if he made another move. I was hoping he'd move."

In the course of my research I had been staggered by the thought of how many different relationships these girls had. I knew that top-priced call girls had one or two paid dates a day. Pony-girls had as many as time allowed. B-girls coasted with one or two servicemen at a time. Streetwalkers tried being with as many men as they possibly could. But, curiously enough, all the girls I had talked to had been either unwilling or unable to estimate the number of men they had known. I recalled Eileen's telling me that she had counted to fourteen and then stopped counting.

"Her vagueness was no accident," the analyst observed. "She meant just that. And, in time, the figure fourteen may fade from her conscious mind. It is part of the subconscious escape from reality."

Realizing that she is an outcast, the prostitute seldom thinks of home and children except in resisting them. And even if she marries through convenience and has children through inadvertence, these are only minor diversions.

"However," the analyst pointed out, "it is not uncommon for her to have recurring dreams which indicate that this lack in her life is subconsciously what she misses more than anything else."

Contemptuous of women who have married well, she masks her own feelings of guilt by scorning them as prostitutes differing only in price. "You don't have to take money to be a prostitute," a call girl said. "Who are some of these women kidding? They're out for anything they can get however they can get it. This model I know passed herself around on Broadway without getting a part, but finally had better luck in Hollywood. This is an *actress?*"

Although she sneers at respectability, the prostitute, particularly the call girl, is supersensitive in polite society, taking refuge in her off hours with Bohemian artists, writers, actors and would-be intellectuals. There she may be accepted as an off-beat personality, without being a curiosity.

"The prostitute's sensitivity increases as she grows older," the analyst explained. "She is quite aware of disapproval from the beginning, but until she has passed her twenties she is sufficiently outside society to remain untroubled by it. And when she eventually feels troubled she criticizes cheating wives and the John's infidelity to his wife.

"Rationalizing further, she may argue that she was violated or that men are beasts or that she needed money for her family. But distressing things happen to other girls and they go on being secretaries, salesgirls, students, wives and mothers. A girl doesn't have to become a prostitute because she's unhappy. Nothing on earth can make a girl a prostitute if she is strongly motivated by self-respect and the respect of others."

While it is an important factor, promiscuity in itself is not enough to make a girl a prostitute. After a brief but stormy interlude as a call girl, an eighteen-year-old stenographer gratefully went back to her desk to earn less in a week than she had made in a night.

"If it hadn't been for a procurer," the analyst said, "she might not have weakened in the first place. But he was insistent, and her respect motivation was confused by her promiscuity. It was the old story of 'You might as well get paid for what you're giving away.'

"Previously, Kitty had submitted only to young men she found attractive. Unfortunately, being oversexed—

not undersexed, mind you—she found a good many attractive men around.

"One of these, who turned out to be a procurer, kept after her. 'You'll meet the kind of men you've never met before,' he told her. Unfortunately, he was right."

For her first date she was to get $100, the procurer taking half. He led her to the rendezvous, tugging at her sleeve, as she tearfully held back.

It was an unnerving experience. "When I got into the room I saw the ugliest, most repulsive man I had ever seen. He was fat and grubby, like a pig. I couldn't bear the thought of taking off my clothes. I felt so dirty and cheap that I just sat there on the edge of the bed and cried."

The procurer suggested tactfully that she disrobe in the bathroom. "He kept telling me not to be silly. Meanwhile the other man kept taking hundred-dollar bills out of his wallet. Finally, there were five bills on the table. The whole thing got so embarrassing that I decided it would be easier to get it over with and get out. I kept crying all through it. I had never been with anyone before that I hadn't wanted. Later, I went into the bathroom, but no matter how I scrubbed I couldn't get clean."

It never got easier. "Taking money spoiled it for me," Kitty said. "No matter how attractive the man was, he became horrible when I thought of getting paid. I couldn't stop crying. I guess men thought it was passion. To get away from it all, I locked myself in my apartment and wouldn't answer the phone."

Eventually, she attempted suicide. When she came to the analyst she was still tormented by pangs of guilt and fearful of sliding back. The experience had one fortunate result—it ended her promiscuity.

"I couldn't bear the thought"—she shuddered—"of ever being with another man."

Kitty's experience made me think of the promiscuous

B-girls. However, the analyst felt that the B-girl was a special problem. "The B-girl is motivated by a spirit of rebellion, but in this early stage her rebellion is directed primarily against her own family and has not yet been transferred to society in general.

"She is in a state of transition, and when the transition is complete she is a full-fledged prostitute, resenting society and everything it stands for. If she can be properly remotivated in time, there is some hope of saving her."

He thought a while. "Speaking generally, there is no single cause of prostitution. It is a combination of past experiences, current circumstances, and the girl's own interpretation of both. Past experiences may have tended to break down the prostitute's relationship to society or make her feel that it had been broken down. In this way she is conditioned, or made vulnerable, to her environment."

The analyst cited the case of a lonely girl, closely paralleling the case of Eileen described earlier in this book. "After an early life in which our social institutions and her family fail her or so she thinks—she may drift to a big city like New York.

"She takes a job and finds herself in a stratum of society which encourages prostitution. She is caught up in the hurlyburly of an indifferent city where the individual seems insignificant, and she has little or no saving tie of affection with her family or anything in her past."

At this stage, she is particularly susceptible to her new environment, the analyst said, because she is without the family and social restraints which make most of us conform.

"However, once she has openly renounced the standards of ordinary society, she is on her way to 'conforming.' She is a 'working girl,' with stipulated hours and conditions, and she can look around and see a great company of colleagues. At last, she is no longer alone—she has become a member of society."

CHAPTER 15

It is only recently that public officials in New York City have begun to feel that constructive steps can be taken to prevent prostitution. Despite public indifference to prostitution, which has been generally regarded as an inevitable evil, increasing promiscuity among young girls has at last been sufficiently alarming to inspire dramatic action. And at the present time, several avenues are being explored which may not only help the prostitute but protect the society she preys upon.

First and foremost, a revolutionary effort is under way to reach girls before they become confirmed prostitutes. A new court, known as Girls Term, was established in 1950 and is now a working model of what Chief Magistrate Murtagh envisions for New York Women's Court.

There is no stigma of criminal procedure, no prospect of imprisonment. "It is a court," says Magistrate Murtagh, "that seeks to help and not to punish." Girls are brought to the attention of the court not by police but by troubled parents, school officials, or social agencies. They are not charged with a specific offense, no formal complaint is lodged against them.

Girls Term is not like any other court in the world. Every attempt is made to minimize the girl's feeling that she is on trial. The presiding magistrate sits at a desk, rather than on the bench, and he converses with the girl, members of her family, and others concerned.

In 1955, almost 600 girls appeared before the court, about 80 per cent of them on the petition of parents, who admitted that the task of handling their teen-agers was too much for them. In cases where the home is judged to be hopelessly inadequate, the court has the power to take jurisdiction of the child, remove her from the home, place her in a foster home, or send her to one of the rehabilitation schools maintained by the Sisters of the Good Shepherd or other private agencies.

Often the girl is merely rebelling against her family situation and has not yet become promiscuous or prostituted herself. She may have been staying out late, frequenting bars, or conducting an intimate relationship with only one boy—invariably someone of whom her family disapproves. Peter M. Horn, senior presiding magistrate of Girls Term, points out that in this early stage there is a good chance of reaching the girl before her rebellious attitude toward her parents extends to society as a whole.

"Because so many of the parents of these disturbed girls have no idea what's going on in their children's minds—or in their lives—" observes Magistrate Horn, "they have made no intelligent effort to sympathize with or understand their children and are perhaps incapable of it. In many cases the parents are foreign-born and their daughters are restricted by old-fashioned European ideas that are completely incompatible with the freedom enjoyed by their contemporaries at school and elsewhere.

"All this creates a barrier between the girl and her parents, she resenting them and they resenting her. Our job is as much with the parents as with the girl, but if we can't do anything toward improving the home environment, we frequently must take the girl out of it.

"There is a sad lack of proper discipline in many of these homes. Nobody has ever said 'no'—the right way— to some of these girls. They have been shouted and screamed at, but how many times has somebody sat down and patiently explained why they shouldn't do something?"

Sometimes the lack of rapport between parents and

girl startles even the most experienced officials. Magistrate Horn recalled the case of a thirteen-year-old girl who had been brought into Girls Term by her father after she had been caught picking up servicemen. The irate father couldn't understand how a daughter of his could behave that way. "Before we got through with the case," Magistrate Horn said, "we learned from the girl herself that when she was eight years old she had watched her parents have intercourse and had then tried to imitate them with various boys in the neighborhood. When she became old enough, twelve or thirteen, she succeeded in satisfying her curiosity with the man who delivered the groceries and with an uncle.

"Her father denounced this story as a lie, and it was obvious that he was sincere, at least. But on investigation, the girl's story stood up. The indignant father had contributed to his daughter's delinquency and didn't even know it.

"The story had to be checked, of course, because these kids, we have discovered, are rebellious enough against their parents to seek revenge by implicating them in all kinds of incestuous relationships. Sometimes the stories are warranted, sometimes not."

For a better understanding of the girl's problem, Girls Term maintains a staff of probation officers, who follow up each case closely, and a psychiatric clinic, specializing in diagnosis and therapy.

In extreme cases, girls are sent to the rehabilitation schools maintained in Manhattan and Peekskill, N.Y., by the Sisters of the Good Shepherd and the Salvation Army's Wayside Home in Valley Stream, L.I. They show infinite patience in softening the rebelliousness of their charges and bringing about a readjustment to society.

At this stage, according to Chief Probation Officer Dorris Clarke, it is largely a matter of giving the girls the motivation they lack. "These girls aren't so much immoral as amoral. They have no consciousness of doing wrong. They don't have the standards of normal girls. It is our job to motivate them and give them standards acceptable to society. With some, we can appeal to a need for self-respect or the respect of others. Some we can interest in preparing themselves for marriage and motherhood. It varies with the girl and her background, and each case requires special understanding and care.

"Sometimes, all that is needed is for someone to show sympathy, listen to the girls' problems, and not look down on them. It is important for them to know that somebody wants them."

Yet, despite her age, by the time a girl has become a prostitute, the spirit of rebellion is already so strong that it is no longer confined to the family circle but strikes out at all authority. Recently, a dramatic case came to the attention of Girls Term. It concerned a sixteen-year-old who was waging a one-girl war on society.

"She had been working out of a rooming house," the case worker declared, "and had five men lined up for that day, at two dollars each, when she was turned over to us. Her family background was bad. An unhealthy relationship with her uncle at the age of thirteen had started her off, followed by the usual promiscuity in the neighborhood, which eventually branched out. She was sent to Villa Loretto, at Peekskill. Since she was infected with syphilis when she entered, she was placed in the infirmary.

"She was a heavy smoker. In an effort to break her of the habit, it was decided to limit her to three cigarettes a day. When she had had her three, she asked for another. This was denied and she began to storm. Later, however, she quieted down, and it was thought that she was becoming tractable. That night she set fire to the infirmary and burned it down. Her war on society cost the State fifty thousand dollars."

While the Girls Term approach holds hope for the future, society's hypocrisy in dealing with the problem stands in the way of any far-reaching reform. Very little headway has been made toward the reform of confirmed prostitutes, and most officials believe that prevention should take precedence over cure. "For the confirmed prostitute," points out Chief Magistrate Murtagh, "our judicial techniques and modern science can contribute little to a solution." When English police, in a new effort to eliminate streetwalking in London, made a visit to New York to see how the police problem was being handled here, they returned home with the comfortable feeling that they were not alone in their bewilderment. "Study what we are doing with streetwalkers," Magistrate Murtagh told them, "if you want to know how not to handle the problem."

We still have a nineteenth-century approach to the problem as a whole, Murtagh feels. "It is incredible," he says, "that night after night police officers accompany these broken-down derelicts to hotel rooms to witness, if not to encourage, their disrobing."

And after the prostitute is arrested and brought to justice, what then?

"In Women's Court," said the Chief Magistrate, "we have nothing to offer the habitual offender but a revolving-door process. We are spending our money for apprehension and punishment, and not a penny for the rehabilitation of prostitutes. We are running a hospital without doctors. A court that punishes the prostitute for finding herself in an unfortunate position is no answer to the problem she creates."

And Magistrate Murtagh is not alone in this opinion. There is a growing awareness among other magistrates that the prostitute is a sick woman who should be treated for her sickness rather than sent off to jail to be corrupted further. Murtagh proposes that prostitution be made a civil offense, with prostitutes committable to a city-owned rehabilitation center where psychiatric care and vocational training would be provided.

Meanwhile, only one-fifth of the girls brought into Women's Court actually serve sentences, and arrests have dropped from 5,000 to 2,000 a year as police concentrate on keeping the girls from operating in public.

And there appears little indication that public education has progressed sufficiently for the problem to be met squarely on all sides. Because of traditional taboos, prostitution many not be mentioned by name on TV or radio even when it is the subject under discussion. Even social workers wrinkle their noses when a prostitute is added to their case load and many religious groups shrink from helping these "sinners."

"We should be the first to raise them up," the pastor of a fashionable Park Avenue church told me, "but how could we take them into our social centers? The mothers would worry about the influence on their daughters, and"—he smiled—"on their husbands."

"The public," contends Miss Clarke, "must change its own schizophrenic, or ambivalent, attitude toward the prostitute—on the one hand, sweeping the problem under the rug, and on the other, putting the entire blame on the women, who are no more criminal than alcoholics or drug addicts.

"If society wants to attribute guilt, then it should attribute guilt equally. Why, if such activity is a crime, should it always be the woman who pays? It is obviously absurd to pick up the girl and do nothing about the customer.

"One of the best ways of discouraging prostitution, I should think, would be by discouraging the customer. I don't say throw him in jail, necessarily, but let him have his share of publicity. I have repeatedly asked male judges: 'What did the girl do that the male wasn't guilty of?'

"If it's the institution of prostitution and the degradation of the individual that we disapprove, then why don't we concentrate on trying to help that individual? Apparently, all we disapprove is the girl."

In other parts of the world, this approach appears to be bearing fruit. In South Viet Nam, police have stripped Dai La Thien, Saigon's plushest bordello, of its mirrors and nude murals and turned it into a school where former prostitutes are being taught sewing, nursing, and other skills. And to discourage relapses, police are under orders to jail any would-be customers who try to tempt girls out of retirement. In a note of Oriental whimsey, offending married males are to be jailed pending application by their wives for their release.

Few are willing and able to give prostitutes a helping hand. And the prostitutes' own disinterest and apathy frequently discourage assistance. The Salvation Army, which has long offered a vocational program for prostitutes, reports that the girls who have responded with interest and later found jobs are rare exceptions.

"The great problem," says Major Dorothy Berry, "is tearing them away from people who have helped get them in trouble. Unfortunately, most of the girls are so disturbed that training them for anything is close to impossible."

The majority, turning to prostitution at an early age, have no trade or profession, she points out, except that which brought about their downfall. "What kind of job can I get—scrubbing floors?" they ask. "Why, I can get more in one night than your job will pay in a month."

"But even more than a job, these girls need somebody to show interest in them. We called one girl's home in Ohio, as she had said she would like to go home. I talked to the girl's mother. We were willing to provide the railroad fare to send the girl back. The mother told us to save our money. She didn't want the girl back under any circumstances. How can you tell a girl, already at the end of her rope, anything like that?

Major Berry, like the analyst, stressed the prostitute's

need for a feeling of belonging to society, even though it may only be a society of other prostitutes.

It almost seems that those who have experienced the despair of being outcasts are the only people who can give prostitutes their hearts. Recently, a group of women, former convicts but never themselves prostitutes, opened a haven for female derelicts in Brooklyn. They called themselves the Ministering Friends.

"It is not enough that a jail door opens to let a prisoner out," the Friends declare. "A door must open to let her in. These women need faith in someone, but most of all they need someone to have faith in them."

THE END

· ·

"The time will come, and soon I hope, when Brotherhood Week will be a reminder, not of the presence of discrimination in our midst, but of its eradication." — **BERNARD BARUCH**

· ·

*The Largest, Most Up-To-Date
And Comprehensive Dictionary
Published In Pocket-Size Format*

WEBSTER'S NEW
WORLD DICTIONARY
of the American Language
(Popular Library Pocket-Size Edition)

Specially prepared for POPULAR LIBRARY
by the expert editorial staff of The World
Publishing Company, universally recognized as
one of the world's leading publishers of
dictionaries, this volume offers to readers in
all walks of life the easiest-to-use word
reference book in this format.

Complete with etymologies, specific examples
to illuminate definitions, idiomatic phrases
and slang terms, full-scope definitions covering
all common usages of words, and a
generous three-line pronunciation key on
every double page spread, it is based
on The College Edition of Webster's New
World Dictionary of the American
Language, which is widely recommended and
used at more than 1,000 American
colleges and universities.

*A Popular Library
Special*